THE
TENDER
SHEPHERD

THE TENDER SHEPHERD

JOHN KILLINGER

Abingdon Press
Nashville

The Tender Shepherd

Library of Congress Cataloging in Publication Data

KILLINGER, JOHN.
  The tender shepherd.
  1. Pastoral theology. I. Title.
BV4011.K55   1985   253   84-24511

ISBN 0-687-41242-0

Scripture quotations unless otherwise noted are from the Revised
Standard Version of the Bible, copyrighted 1946, 1952, 1971, © 1973, by
the Division of Christian Education of the National Council of the
Churches of Christ in the U.S.A., and used by permission.

Those noted KJV are from the King James Version of the Bible.

The excerpt on pages 180-81 is from "An Amicable Divorce" by Mary
McDermott. Copyright 1971 Christian Century Foundation. Reprinted by
permission from the May 5, 1971, issue of *The Christian Century*.

The personal letters printed throughout the book are used by permission of
the letter writers.

Permission has been granted by the persons whose names are mentioned.

MANUFACTURED BY THE PARTHENON PRESS AT
NASHVILLE, TENNESSEE, UNITED STATES OF AMERICA

Contents

Gretis

85718

For the loving members and staff
of First Presbyterian Church of Lynchburg, Virginia,
and especially
my extraordinary secretary,
Mrs. Jean Moyer,
without whom this book
would never have been written

Introduction

I hope this is not the only book, or the best one, the reader will find on the subject, for it is by no means exhaustive or definitive. It is only a sketch, a foretaste, of a book that needs to be written.

It grew out of a situation I found myself in when I returned to the parish ministry after fifteen years of teaching in a seminary. I needed to know something about pastoring.

I was relatively comfortable about my skills in pastoral counseling; even as a teacher I had done a lot of that. I thought I knew a great deal about administration, as I had once been the academic dean of a college. And I certainly was not worried about handling the liturgy and preaching, for these were the areas of my supposed expertise in the seminary.

But pastoring was another matter.

Years before, prior to teaching, I had pastored several small churches, and from that I knew something about human relationships and congregational politics. But now I was going to a large church as the senior minister, the one responsible for programming, pastoral care, budgets, spirituality, outreach, everything. How does one function successfully in a position such as that?

I was uneasy about it and thought a good book would help. But I couldn't find the book I wanted. There were books on small groups and books on church budgets. There

[7]

were books on evangelism and books on missions. There were books on intrastaff relationships and books on managing volunteers. There were books on conducting business meetings and books on providing spiritual nourishment. In short, there were books on just about every subject imaginable, save one. I couldn't find a general book about pastoring, one that would set before me simple pictures of what I ought to be doing for people beyond conducting worship, administering a program, and seeing that the church survived from day to day as a theological entity and a responsible fiscal organization.

What I needed was something very basic, a book filled with suggestions about how to get people involved in their church's ministry and how to make them feel good about their church relationship so they would work together on their spiritual journeys. I needed a book that would stimulate my own thinking about what a pastor can do to evoke a spirit of fellowship and commitment within a congregation. It didn't have to be comprehensive—the older I get, the more I fear straitjackets—but it did have to point me in some welcome directions.

If such a book existed, I didn't find it.

But struggling to make my own way in the parish, I kept thinking about a remark made by Mickey Spillane, one of the pioneers of the hard-boiled detective novel. "I write the kind of books I want to read," he said, "but can't find." Did I dare do the same thing? Was I willing to take a stab at writing the kind of book I couldn't find? My credentials were not right for it. There were hundreds of pastors far more experienced and more gifted than I for doing it. Yet the task would not quit my mind, and I finally had to succumb to it.

Perhaps, if I made no boast of knowing what I was doing, people would not be angry with me for failing.

And perhaps, if I could reveal something of my own wrestling with the problem of how to become a true pastor, it might provide the inspiration for someone else to write the book I couldn't write.

Also, in the meantime, it might help other pastors,

especially young pastors only getting started, to think creatively about pastoral ministry and the way to do it. So here we are, and this book is the result.

A Variety of Churches

Churches vary greatly, of course, and this obviously makes a difference in how they must be pastored.

The church of, say, one hundred to two hundred members is usually quite casual in nature, and the pastor can make drop-in calls on most of the members with fair regularity, catching up frequently on their life stories and responding in rather direct ways to their individual needs. In my first parish, which was only a weekend assignment, I could spend one Sunday afternoon every three months with almost everyone in the congregation by attending the big family dinners to which I was invited. In another parish, where I lived in a parsonage next to the church building, I found it easy to call in every home within a period of only eight weeks. If anyone in these parishes was having a personal problem, I generally knew about it. If anyone was disenchanted with the church and its programs, or wanted to get involved in some new outreach project, I soon found out. I am sure I botched a lot of pastoral opportunities, for I was young and inexperienced. But pastoring in such churches where the minister can maintain a one-on-one relationship to all the members is a relatively simple matter.

Things become more complicated in a church of five or six hundred members, especially if the church cannot afford an additional pastor. The pastor must depend on a pastoral committee or other artifice to discover personal needs as they emerge in the congregation, and then spend time visiting in particular situations. Programming is often difficult, for, while the congregation is large enough to need a great deal of it, trained personnel to supervise it are often lacking. The networking that often functions in larger churches to relate individuals to small groups is incomplete, and the mid-sized church lurches along more or less in the pattern of the smaller church, but with more personal needs unmet. The importance of a pastoral methodology becomes increasingly apparent.

The large church, with a thousand or more members, has been called a *corporation* church. Though many of its members still idealize it in terms of the small rural or neighborhood church, with everyone directly related to the pastor, it obviously cannot operate in this way. The pastor or pastors simply do not have the time or ability to visit regularly with every person and oversee the spiritual welfare of each individual. Networking with pastoral groups and committees becomes essential, and there are inevitably some persons who never meet the pastor in a setting more intimate than the worship service or the seminar room.

Communication, in such a church, is invariably problematic. How does one learn that Mrs. Smith is ill at home, or that Mr. Jones is suffering from a mid-life crisis? How does one keep abreast of what is happening in the lives of all the high school students or tune in to the fears and anxieties of all the senior citizens? I am sometimes embarrassed, as a pastor, to learn that one of my members has moved to another city without my knowing it, or that someone's sister or brother has died after an illness of which I was not aware.

After three years in my present parish, I estimate that I know 10 percent of my congregation at a very intimate level, 20 percent at a more or less intimate level, 30 percent at a casual level, and 20 percent at a mere recognition level. Sad to say, there are probably 20 percent whom I would not know if I met them in the drugstore or supermarket.

How can I possibly pastor the people at the lower end of this scale? Yet pastor them I must, in some fashion. It is part of my calling and part of my yearning. I sincerely *want* to be their pastor.

Finding ways of doing it is part of what this book is about.

Introduction

Basic Human Needs

One thing pastors can count on is that, whatever the size of the church, people are pretty much the same everywhere. That is, they are motivated by the same drives, haunted by the same fears, inspired by the same ideals, lifted by the same hopes. Within any congregation, regardless of size or class or racial composition, there are many people whose needs are basically like those of people in all other congregations.

People are *lonely*. They yearn for approval and companionship. Even with telephones and automobiles, they feel cut off from society. They do all kinds of things to counteract the loneliness and boredom—write letters to the editor of the local newspaper, dream up imaginary complaints for their doctors, and call in persons to service appliances that are working perfectly. One young man in our congregation, who is highly intelligent but has been unable to hold a job, "cruises" the church. He drives past it dozens of times a day, and occasionally stops long enough to walk through the corridors, peering in offices to see who is there. I think of him as standing for all the other church members in their hunger for love and relationship.

Some people are *angry and resentful*. They are dealing with old wounds that never heal—with having been "labeled" as children in school, with never having been accepted and stroked by parents, with some great disappointment in love or career. I once had a woman in a parish who was an absolute bear. She had a reputation for chewing up everyone who got in her way. One day I learned that she had been abandoned by her parents as a small girl and raised by foster parents. Then she married a man who was often unfaithful to her. As she grew older she developed a façade of strength and peevishness. When I knew this, I was able to get close to the woman and to deal wth her as the lonely, frightened, and angry person she really was. After that, there was always a sparkle of gentleness in her eyes when she looked at me,

[11]

even when there was brittleness in her voice. And I have remembered her each time I have encountered a bitter, angry person in subsequent parishes.

Many people are also *bewildered and anxious*. Life in our times is overwhelming for them. They are having to cope with revolutions in life-style that come too quickly to be absorbed. They see the world becoming automated and computerized, and understand little or nothing of the process that now governs their daily existence. One psychiatrist said that he saw at least four new patients who came to him as a result of the breakup of AT&T. In each case, the person experienced deep anxiety over a rearrangement of billing patterns. The psychiatrist said it was symptomatic of general anxiety over a network of operations that affected the patients but was obviously beyond their control. One pastor told me that several persons in his congregation had vigorously resisted his church's acquiring a computer on the grounds that the church ought to be one place in society where those "damnable machines" cannot "take over everything."

Computers and other machines of course represent only one segment of a world that seems to be out of control. The daily news, relayed instantly by wire and satellite, bombards us with the problems and crises of people and nations all over the globe, saturating us, in effect, with depressing awareness of people's moral and physical instability. Acts of terrorism, armed aggression, and the specter of nuclear holocaust haunt the unconscious mind even when banished there by pills and parties and soap operas.

As a result, many people who come to church are not only bewildered and anxious; they are also *eager for some kind of religious solution* to their bewilderment and anxiety. They want to know that "God's in his heaven—all's right with the world." This is one reason for the great resurgence of popular religion in recent decades. When the clergy speak in hesitant tones about the documentary hypothesis regarding the origin of scripture and describe Almighty God as "the Ground of all being" and the process of creation, many people will turn to simpler voices calling for a return to the old-time religion and the unalloyed dogmatism of the days before Darwin, Wellhausen, and Freud. "When I come to church," said one man, "I do not want to hear opinions and theories; I want to hear that 'the Lord God omnipotent reigneth'!"

Part of the problem is that life in the era of the computer has become so secularized that people no longer know how to interpret it with religious under-standing. One young woman who came to see me said that she felt guilty because she no longer knew what she believed about God. When she said she was seeing a psychologist, I asked her if she had talked with the psychologist about this. "No," she said, "I have never had the feeling that she believes anything, so I have been afraid to bring it up." The young woman accepted her therapist's avoidance of religious language or question-ing as normative in an increasingly secularized world, and this enhanced her own confusion about the place of belief in such a world.

This is the kind of world our people live and operate in. They are baffled by changes, upset by their inability to perform or get it all together, depressed by world prospects, and driven into the corner by social and economic pressures. They long to be related to other people, but operate out of fears and inhibitions that spring from bad experiences. They come to church looking for a word of help, and either don't understand what is being said or detect that it is only another form of propaganda in a world that is teeming with propaganda. They try to relate to the congregation but feel over-whelmed by numbers or cliqueishness or the sense that they are never a part of the important decisions, all of which are made when they are not present. They need service and growth opportunities but never seem to have the time to take advantage when they come. They need to be noticed and stroked, but seldom put themselves out in such a way as to receive what they need. They require a larger and clearer vision of their world and its future, and of their own commitment to Christ in the world, but everything about their way of life and their habits of dealing with existence seems to militate against it. These are the people we serve. These are some of the problems they share.

The Call to Be Shepherds

What is our role in their lives? We are their pastors, their priests, their spiritual mediators. Of all the persons they know, we are in the best position to bring order to their troubled outlooks and peace to their restless souls. We stand at the center of the congregation, and, if we can somehow help them become involved with the congregation in the right way, they can find healing and relationship and joy.

The people nearest us at the center usually fare all right. It is the ones on the periphery who need the most care, who stand in the most danger of being lost to the church and its ministries. The artful pastor, said Phillips Brooks, will track the edges like a sheep dog, herding the strays in toward center.

It is the business of caring for the people on the periphery that tests our real pastoral concern. It is easy to care about the people close to us, the ones who invite us to dinner and share their lives with us in every conceivable way. But it is not always easy to care about the ones who dart in and out of church as if they were racing through a stoplight and afraid of being caught. Often, we know too little about them to feel any emotional involvement in their lives. They are mere names and faces to us; or, what is worse, faces without names.

A pastor in Oklahoma City told me about meeting a man who said he had been attending the pastor's church for three years. The pastor was dumbfounded; he could not remember ever seeing the man. "I don't understand," he said to the man; "I thought I knew almost everybody in the congregation. How is it that I have never met you before?" The man explained. He is a psychiatrist who deals with people and their problems five days a week. On Sunday, he wants to worship but does not wish to be with people. He comes to church, sits behind some large plants at the rear of the contemporary sanctuary, and slips out before the benediction.

Perhaps this man is capable of dealing with his world without additional involvement in the congregation. But many persons are not. They need the care of the pastor or his or her surrogates within the church, who will help them to relate to Christ's church as a whole, so that they draw strength and inspiration from it. They need to experience Christ as he is mediated through those who are living together in his presence and making sense of their world through his teachings. In other words, they need pastoring, shepherding.

The Gospels contain many beautiful pictures of Christ and his disciples. But there is none that haunts me as pleasantly as the one in which he and Peter are walking by the seashore after the resurrection. Peter has been through a rough time, betraying the Lord to whom he was devoted. Then, filled with the wonder of Easter, he has traveled with the other disciples back to Galilee, back to the lake in whose waters he wet his feet as a child. During the night they have fished and caught nothing, as though some divine power—or alien influence—were controlling the deeps. At daybreak, as the light filters in around the horizon of the world, a voice calls to them from the shore, "Children, have you any fish?" "No," they reply emptily. "Cast the net on the right side of the boat, and you will find some." They do, and lo, the net strains with the flipping, slithering bodies of dozens of large fish. "It is the Lord!" says the youngest disciple. And Peter, possibly the oldest, slips into his tunic and strikes out for shore, not willing to wait for the rest.

There is the breakfast, fresh fish and bread, cooked over an open fire. And then the walk along the shore.

"Simon, son of John," says Jesus, using his most intimate name, "do you love me more than these?"

"Yes, Lord; you know that I love you." Words of contrition; a voice probably filled with remorse and apology.

"Feed my lambs."

Three times.

And each time the same, or nearly so. "Feed my lambs." "Tend my sheep." "Feed my sheep."

It was the pastoral charge, given by one who only a few days before had said, "The good shepherd lays down his life for the sheep."

How does any pastor ever wrest free from the charge? It is always there, night and day, riveting, dogging, accusing, inspiring.

Perhaps it is why Dean Inge of St. Paul's said he could get no rest, even after he retired, for thinking of all the things he had left undone.

And it is why we must always wrestle with the pastoral task of feeding the sheep, of herding them in toward center, where there is warmth and security, of leading them beside still waters, of bringing them safely into the presence of the Good Shepherd himself. The task is never done. Our imaginations and energies are rarely up to it. But we must keep trying, keep looking for ways to do it.

To that end, this book is dedicated. And it is only a beginning.

I

Reaching Out and Touching Everyone

"Reach out and touch someone," invites a famous long-distance telephone advertisement. The most immediate need I felt, on moving to a large parish, was to reach out and touch *every*one. There were approximately twelve hundred people in my congregation. They had had a succession of four pastors and an interim pastor in a period of only twelve years. In some ways, they were almost a *non*-congregation. Some seven or eight hundred of them crowded into the sanctuary on Sunday morning for worship, and perhaps a hundred and fifty took time after the service to move through the line and greet the pastor. But, apart from the old families whose fathers and mothers had sustained the church for generations, they had no real sense of togetherness. They were sheep who had had too many shepherds in too brief a time. I wanted to put my arms around them, get to know them all, speak to them individually, give them a feeling of assurance. But how?

Fortunately, there was an old congregational directory that had been put together several years before. The photographs were out of date, but they were still helpful to a new pastor trying to learn his flock. I worked at getting names and faces together and planned my visiting to include persons I could not remember having met at church. And one of my first official actions as the pastor was to call for a new directory, a desideratum that in a church the size of ours required about eight months to fulfill.

In the meantime, I surveyed the means presently used to communicate with the congregation. They included a weekly mailing of the church bulletin, occasional letters to the congregation, and a monthly newsletter that was about as interesting as a spare-parts catalog.

A Weekly Newsletter

Soon we dispensed with the mailing of the bulletin and replaced it with a weekly newsletter, one that we hoped had personality as well as information. We announced that it would be initiated, and asked the congregation to suggest names for it. From the dozen or so names put forward, a poll led us to settle on *First Press,* and soon the new publication was born. At first it was the effort of the pastor, the pastor's wife, and the pastor's secretary, but later an editorial board of volunteers was formed and now meets weekly at the church to plan and lay out the issues.

Church newsletters vary greatly in appearance and content. Some are expensively printed on slick paper, others turned out on old mimeograph machines. We decided that ours would be attractively designed and printed on the church duplicating machine. This would be cheaper, would involve more volunteers in production, and would permit us to work closer to deadline with information and materials.

For pastors planning new newsletters, or thinking of revamping old ones, I suggest the following checklist of desirable qualities:

1. A church newsletter should be *neat*. The typing should be as faultless as possible, margins should be even, and the overall production should carry a sense of competency and efficiency.

2. A church newsletter should be *attractive*. A pleasant arrangement of material, with plenty of white space, nicely lettered titles, and pleasant little reproductions of drawings or pictures, helps make it readable. Booklets of

useful drawings are available from several sources, and an alert secretary will maintain a "morgue" or file of such drawings clipped from newspapers and other newsletters.

3. A church newsletter should be *informative*. It ought to carry as much useful and up-to-date material on church activities as possible, as well as on related activities in the community. For some time, we included in our letter a monthly calendar of all church activities, but later abandoned this for a weekly calendar that is fuller and more accurate.

4. A church newsletter should be *accurate*. All dates and times should be double-checked for accuracy, as should spellings of names and information about various programs and happenings.

5. A church newsletter should be *interesting*. The writing should be fresh and crisp. Reports of meetings and programs should sparkle with a special quality. Feature articles should prove absorbing and captivating. There is nothing worse than a dull newsletter!

6. A church newsletter should be *warm and personal*. There is enough impersonal printed material entering our homes every day through the mail and the newspaper. When the church is trying to build a sense of community in the congregation, it is essential that the newsletter be an expression of community, that it be caring and stroking and personable. I receive newsletters from at least a dozen churches each week. Most of them go directly into the wastebasket. But there are two or three I invariably read because they convey a sense of warmth and love. Even though I am not a member of the congregations they represent, I feel as if I am. These newsletters make me feel included.

The Pastor's Paragraph

The most conspicuous spot in each issue of *First Press* is devoted to the "Pastor's Paragraph." I am convinced, after four years of feedback from parishioners, that this paragraph is, moment for moment, the most important

FIRST PRESS

Published by
First Presbyterian Church, Lynchburg, Virginia

Vol. III   December 16, 1982   No. 40

PASTOR'S PARAGRAPH

Dear Friends:

One of the beautiful things about Christmas is the feeling of "family" it evokes. People who are normally Scrooges with each other find themselves reaching out in friendship. The rich have thoughts of tenderness toward the poor, and everybody wants to embrace everybody else in a time of good will and generosity. So what, if Madison Avenue tries to capitalize on it? Maybe the merchandizing helps to spread the feeling. The important thing is a sense of oneness, of being drawn together by the imagery of shepherds and wisemen congregating together to worship the Babe of Babes in a simple manger. Those of us who work around the church want you to know how much we feel that you are "family" at this time of year. As we review the year, and remember all the times we have seen you and shared life with you, sometimes in joy and sometimes in sadness, we are grateful to God for being part of you. We hope you have a beautiful Christmas, whether here with us or off at a distance, and that it will be a time of deepening peace and inward renewal for you, as it is meant to be. May the One who was born at Bethlehem reign triumphantly in your hearts, is our prayer and holiday wish.

Affectionately,

John Killinger

CHRISTMAS MUSIC AND DRAMA

On Sunday at 7:30 p.m. the Chancel Choir will perform Antonio Vivaldi's "Gloria in Excelsis Deo", with soloists Libby Jarrett and Myrna Blake (soprano) and Joyce Bailey (mezzo-soprano). The "Gloria" was sung by the choir for the first time in this church in 1969 and prompted the purchase of the harpsichord, to be used again on Sunday.

Following the choral work, the Youth and Children's Choirs will combine, under the direction of Suzanne Currie, in an adaptation of "A Swiss Nativity."

We do hope you will show your appreciation of the work and artistry which have gone into this expression of Christmas on the part of our choirs. Music and drama represent a two-way street -- performers give a great deal of themselves but they need an audience to receive what they have to give! So, y'all come and we promise you an evening to remember.

December 19

The fourth candle of Advent is lit to center our thoughts on God's great gift of Love and Hope.

Scripture lessons: Micah 5:1-4
                      Luke 1:39-47

Wreath lighting ceremony:

9:00 a.m. service: Nanci and Jeff Gould, Jonathan and MacGregor

11:00 a.m. service: Hilda and Elliott Gentry, Carolyn Gentry

investment of my time as a pastor. It rarely takes more than half an hour to write—sometimes only fifteen minutes—yet it is read (and often cited) by most of the adults in our congregation.

It is part gossip column, part humorous essay, part propaganda piece, part devotional thought, and part inspirational message. In Lent, it inclines to instruction and meditation; in stewardship season, to challenge and a rethinking of our giving patterns. It is a *personal* word—what *I* am thinking, how *I* am feeling, what *I* believe—yet always turned toward the care and self-interest of my people. And it is a *promotional* word, promoting fellowship, Christian values, and our church's program.

Here are some briefer examples (program-pushers often run a little longer):

Wow! Did you see the Cincinnati Bengals-San Diego Chargers game on TV last Sunday afternoon? There were 50,000 fans in those bleachers, with the temperature *minus* 10 and a wind-chill factor of 60 below. Talk about dedication! There were frostbite stations at several locations in the coliseum, with numerous doctors and paramedics in attendance, and city buses were drawn up at warming stations for fans who needed a bit of respite. I couldn't help wondering, as I watched, what could be done to infuse that kind of commitment into Christians for the work of God's kingdom. It makes you think, doesn't it? We say Christ is the most important thing in the world to us. But do we really behave as if he were? I don't mean to chide you—or me—only to suggest that we need to reconsider our degree of commitment from time to time. This week is a good time to do it, as we prepare our Commitment Forms to be turned in during the worship service next Sunday. Maybe, when the ushers are carrying those forms down to the communion table as an act of congregational dedication, we'll remember the Bengals-Chargers game and say to ourselves, "By golly, I want to be that devoted to Christ this year!"

One of my Christmas presents was a desk calendar with daily sayings based on Murphy's Law and similar pronunciamentoes—billed as "365 reasons why things go Ɡuoɹʍ!" Some of the sayings are worth pondering. For example—January 7, Murphy's Sixth Corollary: "It is impossible to make anything foolproof because fools are so ingenious." January 25, Issawi's Law of Progress: "A shortcut is the longest distance between two points." February 3, Zymurgy's First Law of Evolving Systems Dynamics: "Once you open a can of worms, the only way to recan them is to use a larger can." I cheated and looked ahead to see what is up for December 31, the last day of the year. It is called "The Last Law," and says: "If several things that could have gone wrong have not gone wrong, it would have been ultimately beneficial for them to have gone wrong." Who says there is no theology in contemporary life? But how much better I like the words of the Apostle Paul: "We know that in everything God works for good with those who love him, who are called according to his purpose." We might call that Paul's Proclamation. Have a good day!

In one of our services a couple of weeks ago, I made a little pleasantry about our choir's having given up English for Lent. I thought about that later. Some people, I know, do not like to hear Latin anthems; they are bothered by language they cannot understand. But it occurred to me that Latin anthems help to offset our Protestant word-dependency—the tendency in some churches to suspect anything that cannot be reduced to a formula or statement. We Presbyterians are especially prone to make idols of words. John Calvin wanted church buildings cleared of all icons and images—everything except scripture verses printed on the walls. Some Presbyterian churches still have large-print verses painted in their sanctuaries. Yet life is much more than words; it is gesture, mime, feeling, dance, and dream. The presence of Christ transcends all words; it is something felt, something touched, something known in the depths of our beings. Why not, then, have musical spaces in our services when words do not predominate? Certainly they are welcomed by those right-brained people for whom images are more important than creeds and doctrines. So relax, if you've always thought you despised Latin anthems; "see" the pictures being painted for worship; let the music touch something deeper than words.

Well, it finally happened to me! Last Saturday I was on my way from the church to the post office, with half a dozen other errands on my mind as I drove along. When I came to Virginia

[22]

Reaching Out and Touching Everyone

Baptist Hospital, I automatically turned into the drive and looked for a parking space. Lo and behold, there was one right in front. Bingo! I thought, this is the first time this week I've managed to get a space, and right in front too! I turned off the engine and started to get out, when I thought, I'm not going to the hospital, I'm going to the post office! I chuckled as I started the engine, backed up, and drove away. I was remembering a pastor friend in Dunedin, Florida, who was asked to drive his car at the head of a funeral procession. On the way to the cemetery, he switched on his stereo and was listening to the music. He forgot all about the funeral, and, when he came to a K-Mart store and remembered something he needed there, swung into the parking lot and started looking for a space. He happened to glance in the rearview mirror and saw a string of cars following him with their lights on. Oh-oh! he thought, and nimbly guided them all back out to the highway as though nothing had happened. Routines sometimes make us forget important things. Let's remember, during these final weeks of Lent, to take advantage of all the offerings of our church to help us prepare for Holy Week and Easter.

"Lie here, beloved dust, until the joyful dawn." These are the words the Russian novelist Dostoevsky had inscribed on his mother's tombstone. I thought of them several times as we prepared to bury my mother last week. My own theology of life after death does not include an interim sleep—I believe that souls pass instantly to the pleasure of life in God—but the phrase kept recurring in spite of that. I guess it was the "beloved dust" part. That's the way I felt about Mother's body after she died. It still looked like Mother, but it wasn't she; what was really vital about her was gone. One of these days I will share with you some reflections about her death and the funeral. But for now I want to tell you how much your care and sympathy have meant. When I looked across the aisle at the funeral and saw five people from our church sitting there, I was overwhelmed with a sense of your love and support. And your phone calls, cards, and other expressions of sympathy have been wonderful. We are grateful to you for everything you've done, and to God for letting us live among such generous and beautiful people. I hope your ears burn; we brag about you wherever we go!

[23]

As I review these paragraphs, I realize that one of the unconscious rules I have worked by is to keep them as secular as possible. I don't mean that they aren't religious in nature, but that the religion grows naturally out of everyday thoughts or incidents, not out of a prior decision to say something religious. This is important, I believe. Ministers are too often identified as Holy Joes or Janes because they are clergy-persons. Then everything they say is predictable and expected. I often end up at a predictable destination, but I try to begin in unusual places and get there by natural means. This imparts, I hope, a certain freshness, an earthy vitality, to the thoughts I deal with. It also reveals snatches of *me*—of someone personal—for the congregants to relate to.

Letters to Visitors and New Members

Another "low cost" pastoral gesture is the form letter we send to each visitor who signs our register and each new member who joins the church. Sending a letter does not always take the place of a personal visit; the visit may follow. But we make it a point to send the letters as soon as possible and then to follow up with a visit when we can.

The letter to visitors reads something like this:

Dear Friend:

I was happy to see your name in our Friendship Book for last Sunday and to know you visited our congregation. I hope you found the service helpful to you and that we shall have the pleasure of welcoming you back at an early date.

Cordially yours,

Letters to new members usually sound something like this:

Dear First Name:

I feel genuine pleasure in our having received you into the membership of our congregation. We have a warm and outgoing fellowship, as I believe you have been able to see, and it will be all the richer for your having joined it.

Reaching Out and Touching Everyone

Now that I am your pastor, I hope you will not feel hesitant to share with me any particular joys or difficulties that come into your life. I look forward to getting to know you much better.

Yours sincerely,

This letter may appear brief and incomplete, but a fuller letter, mentioning the member's commitment and some of the opportunities available through church membership, was previously included in a packet of new member materials the person received when he or she joined the church. Among the materials were a pictorial membership directory, pamphlets describing Christian education and service opportunities, and a commitment form for surveying the member's talents, interests, and former church service experiences. Information from the form, once collated and passed on to all chairpersons of committees and mission groups, is now being programmed into our computer.

One reason for keeping both of these form letters brief is that each letter is personally typed on our best stationery and personally signed. While we have a word processor as part of our computer center, we believe it is important to retain as much individuality as possible in our dealings with persons who are as yet only marginally acquainted with our congregation.

Friendship Books

I mentioned above the Friendship Book. This is the name we use for the standard sort of attendance books that we use in the pews to track attendance each Sunday. These books were not used when I first came to our church, and initially there was some resistance to using them, primarily from church officers who did not like the idea of "being checked up on." But we eventually broke down the resistance while making a strong effort to establish an Evangelism Mission Group in the church. "It is the best way," we pointed out, "to ensure that we secure the names of all visitors and that our members in the pews with them get to know who they are."

From a pastoral viewpoint, I find the books irreplaceable. In a large congregation with two worship services, it is the only possible way of keeping up with the vagaries in members' attendance, thereby spotting possible difficulties they are having either in their personal lives or with the church. Our first thought was to have a small volunteer committee come in on Monday mornings and collate the attendance sheets with a master record. But our minister of music, whose Monday mornings were relatively free times—"hangover time," he called them—said that he would be happy to do the job, and has done it faithfully and beautifully ever since.

When a member has missed five consecutive Sundays, we flag the name for a telephone call or a visit from one of the pastors or the Pastoral Mission Group. We try not to be heavy-handed. We merely begin with, "We notice you've been absent from worship services for several weeks, and hope nothing's wrong." And then we play it by ear. If there is a problem, we try to help with it. If not, we simply underline the fact that the person is missed.

One woman, a former church officer who had missed four Sundays and was planning to go to the beach the next weekend, was "caught" looking for the Friendship Books in the church office where they are kept and confessed that she wanted to sign her name so no one would check up on her!

The Book of Days

Another form of register we keep is something I call, for want of a better name, "The Book of Days." It is an ordinary notebook which we have turned into a diary or calendar. It is not geared to a specific year, only to the days—January 1, January 2, and so forth. Under these day headings we try to list the anniversaries of births, baptisms, marriages, divorces, promotions, deaths, and other important events in people's lives. By glancing ahead in the book each week, we can determine where a telephone call, a visit, or a letter would be especially welcome.

I try particularly to remember the anniversaries of marriages and deaths, and have developed form letters for my secretary to send if I am going to be away or am otherwise too busy to take care of the occasions personally. The one for marriages says:

Dear First Names,
   Congratulations on the approach of your first anniversary! I know it has been a year of growth, challenge, and excitement for both of you as you have explored the meaning of life together. My prayers are with you as you enter your second year.

                                        Affectionately,

There are three death anniversary letters, one for a child whose parent died, one for parents whose child died, and one for a person whose spouse died. Here is the one for a person whose spouse died:

Dear First Name:
   I know this hasn't been the easiest of years for you, being without _____, and that facing the anniversary of his/her death is one of the hardest things you have to do. Please remember that I am thinking about you and will be holding you in prayer on this special day. May God give you joy in contemplating _____'s blessedness where he/she is, and peace for fulfilling the tasks of your own daily life.

                                        Sincerely,

Again, each letter is personally typed and signed.

Year-End Letters

The week after Christmas is almost invariably quiet around churches as people visit with their loved ones or simply recuperate from all the holiday preparations. I find that it is an excellent time for reviewing the year and giving thanks for certain people who have made unusual contributions to my life or the church's life. After making a list of these persons, I quickly dictate notes of gratitude to them.

A typical year-end letter may say:

Dear Phyllis:

As this year comes to a close and I look back across it for the things that have made it special, nothing stands out more for me than the super job you have done in training our acolytes and seeing that they are always there to do their job on Sunday morning. Nothing in the entire year has added as much to our worship as their presence. I know what a sacrifice of time and effort it has been for you to mastermind this program, and I'm sure I speak for the entire congregation when I say, "Thank you! You have given Sunday mornings just the touch they needed!"

Sincerely,

Perhaps this belongs under the category of "The Care and Feeding of Volunteers," if one wishes to categorize it. It means a great deal to many of those who receive such letters. For example, here is a letter I received in response to such a year-end letter written to a gentleman in his early seventies who had been active in both our Boy Scout and Keenager programs, among others:

Dear Pastor:

Murphy's Law had practically dominated my life for over a week until Thursday when the "opposing forces" moved in swiftly and effectively. On that day my fortune completely changed and for various reasons:

1. Thanks to Almighty God my miserable "cold" had reversed its devastating course and I actually felt right good for a change.

2. Without being asked, my most valued friend called offering to do some grocery shopping and to get my car back in operation.

3. Then later in the day our mailman delivered a letter from my pastor which immediately provided total relief from my accumulated depression.

Your letter was timely, unduly kind, and very deeply appreciated.

My Lord, my valued friend of many years, and my pastor changed my life on Thursday. I wish each knew what their action has meant to me but I just can't adequately explain it.

> Appreciatively,
> Bob Redfern

Few persons ever respond as beautifully as this man did. But I find that sending the letters gives me as much pleasure as it could possibly give those who receive them. I *do* appreciate these special persons, and it is important for me to say so.

Special Telephone Calls

I do not mean to slight Ma Bell and all the other telephone companies. Phone calls can often be as important as letters, and the telephone is the single most important instrument for keeping in touch with parishioners.

I try once a month to take thirty minutes to flip through our membership roster, noting the names of people I think I ought to check up on with a call. The conversations are rarely lengthy. I say, "Hi, I haven't talked to you lately and just wanted to check on you and see how you're doing." Sometimes a call unearths a reason for a visit. Usually, though, it ends as a little chat with a cheery good-bye.

"Meet the Minister"

One of the biggest problems pastors of large congregations have is scheduling—trying to fit the hundreds of things that *must* be done and the hundreds of things that *ought* to be done each week into a practicable time frame.

There are invariable constraints on the minister's time, such as sermon preparation, committee meetings, staff conferences, hospital visitation, weddings, funerals, and counseling appointments. These constraints often conspire to keep halfhearted souls away from the pastor's door or to make it difficult for him or her to visit the homes of couples when both husband and wife can be present.

Frustrated by the sense that I wasn't available to see certain persons because of these constraints, I wondered what I could do to overcome the opportunity gap between us. Was there a time when I could sort of hold open house for them and let them come whenever they felt the desire to do so? I remembered the pastor of a large church in Grand Rapids who told me several years ago that he tried to be in his office one night each week for people merely to drop in on him without an appointment. But my experience had been that most people I tried to call on in the evening were busy or at least pressed for time. Perhaps Sunday mornings would work for many of them. That seemed to be the least-programmed slot of the week, unless they were in Sunday school.

So I settled on the third Sunday morning of each month, from ten till ten forty-five, the hour between our worship services, and gave it the name "Meet the Minister." The week prior to the third Sunday, the church bulletin and the newsletter announce, in effect, "Next Sunday is 'Meet the Minister' Sunday. Our pastor will be in the parlor beside the chancel at 10 A.M. to meet with any persons wishing to discuss church membership or the Christian faith."

Now, on a typical "Meet the Minister" Sunday, I enter the room to find anywhere from three to a dozen persons, most of them inquirers whose schedules would not permit their coming at another hour. I quickly survey them to learn what has brought them there, and then I try to hold a general discussion with all of them, answering particular questions as I go. Although most of them hear things in the process that they already know, I

[30]

figure it is important for them to hear them again from the perspective of this particular pastor and with embellishments that tell them more about our particular church. At the conclusion of our time together, those who wish to become candidates for membership in the church complete the necessary information forms and I make additional appointments with those who for any reason desire or need a subsequent meeting.

Meet the Church Staff

Many people in the average congregation never have a very clear picture of what their church staff members do behind the scenes to make the church function during the week. Some of them see the large figures in the budget for salaries and staff support and wonder how they can be justified. Others imagine that church buildings are relatively inactive places during the ordinary working week and come alive only on the weekends. Recently I had a visit from a young man wanting to talk about entering the ministry. When I asked him about his motivations for doing so, he said, "Well, I'm a quiet, studious person and I would like to work in an unhurried environment." He had no idea what the average church is like during the week.

I think it is important to let people see what their money is paying for and what their staff members are doing during an average work day. Accordingly, we make every attempt to spotlight our various staff members, especially when they are up to something new or difficult. Once, as part of a fall stewardship campaign, we even sent out a three-page letter called "A Day in the Life of Your Church Staff," written in reportorial fashion and describing what all of us were doing at particular times of the day. Here is an excerpt from the middle of the letter:

Ten o'clock finds Dora typing a letter to the Junior High Fellowship, responding to John's call for a telephone number aand stopping mid-letter to copy a sheet of information for one of the W.O.C. officers who needs it

immediately if not sooner. Across the hall, Eloise has
paused in her effort to secure callers for the church
dinners and is going over some quarterly financial
statements with Jean, who is helping collate them.

Norman is reviewing the difficult score of Vaughan
Williams' *Hodie,* which the choir will do in December,
and goes to the piano to pick out the vocal parts. John is
phoning people to serve on a committee that must be
appointed at the next Session meeting, and Bernard is
preparing to go down to the preschool chapel at 10:30 and
give a brief devotional for the children.

About 11:00, Norman is interrupted in his study by a
mother who wishes to discuss the music for her
daughter's wedding. They have a pleasant visit. Norman
makes notes on the family's wishes for the music, and
explains his own theology of wedding music. Jean,
meantime, has completed her work on the financial
statements and has turned to typing a sermon in final
form for printing and distribution to the congregation.
Dora, between phone calls, is typing cards to elders,
deacons, and ushers who are to serve during the coming
month, and Eloise has gone back to her task of forming a
telephone committee for the church dinners.

It is John's day to visit in the hospital, and he is
walking over, meditating on a sermon idea and preparing
himself in prayer for the visits. Bernard, having
completed arrangements for the afternoon visitation, is
now answering mail and reviewing the visitors' cards
placed in the offering plates last Sunday. There are five
church members in the hospital. After spending a few
minutes and having prayer with each of them, John stops
to visit with a nonmember who teaches in a local college.

Lunch finds the troups scattered in several directions.
Dora is holding the fort and answering the phone while
the receptionist is away. Bernard and John are having
lunch separately with businessmen who needed to talk
about personal problems. Eloise has cut some roses from

the rose garden and has stopped by the hospital to deliver them to a patient who was once a member of First Church, then moved away, and has recently returned to live in Lynchburg. Jean is still working on the sermon for the printers, and hopes to get it finished before leaving for lunch. Only a paragraph from the end, she stops a minute to chat with Marge about the day-school accounts, which she will be sending out tomorrow. Norman remains in his office, eating a sack lunch while poring over literature about new music available for choirs and organists.

The letter ends with the last two staff members leaving the building late in the afternoon and commenting on how the trees have turned. They walk toward their cars in the parking lot.

There is a loneliness about their cars sitting there in the parking lot. But it is not the kind of loneliness one feels about cars that sit alone in an industrial or commercial parking lot. It is a sweet, mellow kind of loneliness, that reflects the warmth and friendliness of all the people who have been in and out of the church building during the day, that recalls the voices of the preschoolers playing outside in the morning, that anticipates the crowds of cars to be brought here by eager worshipers on Sunday. A squirrel absentmindedly watches the two cars as they leave. Soon he is left alone, and hops on into the rose garden, where he sits eating a nut from a nearby tree. Dusk gathers. A special aura seems to rest upon the church property.

There are never any remarks in our congregation about how little the staff members do. People know how dedicated and busy they are. And it is important for them to know this. It helps them to feel excited and enthusiastic about their church's work!

Pastoral Self-Interviews

In a similar vein, I sometimes try to communicate my own thoughts on subjects via a "self-interview." It is a trick I picked up from James Dickey, the poet and novelist, who once published an entire volume called *Self-Interviews*. His editors said that the technique provided "a long-needed convenient forum for the poet to say something permanent about his own poetry." The self-interview *is* a convenient forum, for it permits the author or speaker to "set up" the questions he or she deems to be important in the understanding of a subject.

Here, for example, is part of a self-interview I wrote during a time when I was preaching weekly on the Bible and the way it should be read today:

Q.: But when you say the Bible should be read the same way we read a novel, doesn't that diminish the sacred significance of the Bible?

A.: Not really. What I mean is that the Bible should be viewed as *story,* as narrative, so that we read not only what is there but what was going on behind the scenes.

Q.: Between the lines, in other words.

A.: Exactly. I remember an aged minister in South Carolina, a wonderful black preacher, who said that the older he got, the less he read what the Bible said and the more he read between the lines.

The idea is to keep the prose as limpid and casual as it would be in an actual interview or conversation. Humor is particularly advantageous. And I find that in my questioning role I often voice the thoughts and queries that I know are uppermost in some people's minds—like the one above about being disrespectful to the Bible as a sacred book. I have even taken a hard line with myself and demanded better answers than I was getting. This is particularly disarming to readers who would really like to ask such questions of the minister; they become enthusiastic as they read, putting themselves into the questioner's place. Then, when I finally answer the question or, as in some cases, admit that I must do some more thinking on the matter, they have really heard me, for we have worked together in arriving at the conclusion.

This method is especially useful, I believe, for treating sensitive or debatable issues in the parish. It permits people to see that the pastor understands both sides of an issue, not just the one he or she represents, and helps them think through both sides the way the pastor does.

The State of the Church

This chapter is becoming far too long, but that is because communication is the name of so much that we have to do in the parish. People need to know what is going on, they need to be in touch with one another, they need encouragement from the staff, they need to feel that they are part of the action. It is important that all of this becomes a part of the active program of the church, that the ministers and staff make it happen. And it is important that there be an upbeat note in all of it, so that people feel *positively* about the church and its mission.

We have found it extremely helpful, when the year's work is done and we are ready to tackle another year, to provide for our people a succinct and accurate summary of some of the more tangible achievements of the past year. For some years, this took the form of a three- or four-page letter to the congregation called "The Pastor's Annual Report to the Church." Like the President's State of the Union message, it purported to tell people where we were, what we had done, and what we had to look forward to in the coming year. This report included such items as:

Number of new members added to roll
Number of members lost by transfer, death,
   or transferral to inactive roll
Number of persons baptized
Number of children confirmed
Number of weddings and funerals in the church
Average attendance at church school
Special activities and seminars during the year
Staff changes
Performances by the choirs
Work of the Pastoral Mission Group

Work of Community, National, and
  World Missions Groups
Activities of the Women of the Church
Activities of the Keenagers
Financial stewardship
Special fellowship activities
Work done on church property
Acquisition of new equipment
Activities of volunteer groups
  such as receptionists, chancel
  guild, mission volunteers

More recently, we have attempted to *personalize* this report by turning it into the major feature of an all-church dinner held annually in January. Various parts of it are presented, not by the pastor, but by Mission Group chairpersons, W.O.C. officers, staff members, and others more intimately involved in those parts. As the pastor, I have confined my report to items not easily covered by other major reports of the evening. The entire report is recorded on tape and made available to anyone who wishes to hear it again. It is also summarized and placed in the church records.

Once the report is given, the floor is opened for questions, and people are urged to air any concerns they may have about any aspect of the church's life and work. While this kind of openness has been a major feature of annual meetings in some churches, notably the Baptist and Congregational, it is hardly the rule among most congregations. But, properly prepared for and emceed, it is an excellent way of handling worries and complaints and developing a spirit of progress and unanimity in the church.

As we said, communication is the thing. We have to be able to reach out and touch everyone!

II

The Care and Feeding of New Members

One of the most difficult tasks in a larger church is that of assimilating new members. In a small church it can be relatively easy. Everybody is quickly conscious of the presence of Bob and Marcia Neucomer and is probably anxious to make them feel welcome. They, in turn, easily remember the names of the sixty or eighty people who comprise the faithful core of the church's membership, and are soon on a first-name basis with many of them. But in a larger church Bob and Marcia may well feel lost in the masses and overwhelmed by the noise and strangeness of the hordes of people they encounter every Sunday in their new congregational family.

"It's like working in a Cecil B. De Mille movie," said one man who had recently joined a church of fourteen hundred members. "You walk around in a crowd of thousands and never recognize a single person!"

Studies have shown that new members not integrated into some small group or functioning unit of the church within six months of joining will probably be lost to the church before the first year is out. Therefore every effort must be expended to incorporate them as quickly as possible.

A Warm Beginning

When I came to my present church, the new-member process, begun after the pastor had interviewed persons desiring to join the church, called for an all-too-brief meeting of the candidates with part of the Session or Board of Elders sandwiched into five or ten minutes between the nine o'clock worship service and church school. They were introduced, voted on, prayed over, and all but trampled in the rush to get to Sunday school classes and various duties around the building. Then they were introduced by the pastor at the eleven o'clock service and more or less abandoned to the Lord and the future for their fate as good church members.

Our process now is primarily an expansion of the one then, and I hope it is only a step toward a much better method, but at least it is an improvement. Once candidates for membership have been identified and visited, they are invited to meet the Session. Early in the week before this meeting takes place, they receive a letter reminding them of the meeting, containing salient information such as the time and location, and generally outlining again the process that will take place during and following the meeting. On Sunday morning, they are greeted at the door by an elder and presented with name tags which they are asked to wear for the remainder of the morning.

The pastor or associate pastor calls the meeting to order and offers a prayer. The purpose of the meeting is outlined and those seeking membership are introduced, often with some personal word about their families, where they attend school or are employed, and other information. The elders vote on their candidacy and they are welcomed into our fellowship. They are presented with membership packets that include a letter of greeting, a pictorial directory of church members, pamphlets about the church and the educational opportunities we offer, a stewardship card, and a commitment form. The Commitment Form, which they are urged to complete and return to the church office as soon as possible, is an inventory of their experiences, talents, and preferences for places of service in the church. The information from each form is immediately translated into our computer system and passed on to the chairpersons of various mission groups, committees, task forces, and other organizations in the church so that the chairpersons can contact them and get them involved in appropriate segments of the church's life.

The new members are told about the nature of our church as a large institution and the importance of their becoming involved in smaller units within it. They are invited to the next fellowship dinner and apprised of other fellowship opportunities in the church. They are also urged to attend a program of four orientation sessions and told when these sessions will begin and where they will be held. Finally, they are introduced to their sponsors in the church family, who will befriend them and help them to become integrated into our life and programs over the next several months.

Following a prayer by one of the elders, there is a brief time of greeting and exchange among all of those present, and all the new members are photographed so that their pictures may be displayed in our "New Member Gallery," an attractive display case mounted on the wall in the foyer outside the sanctuary and narthex.

Our nine o'clock service has been moved back to eight forty-five, so that we now have an unhurried fifteen or twenty minutes for this process instead of the five or ten minutes we formerly had. Ideally, we should have thirty or forty minutes—time to introduce each new member in more depth and time for everyone to visit in a more leisurely fashion. We have even considered following the practice of some churches and receiving new members in the evening, when an entire hour could be given to the process. But we find that most teenagers and adults, in these busy times, simply cannot manage a separate evening as well as they can manage the time on Sunday morning. So we transact the necessary business on Sunday morning and try to provide supplementary occasions of an optional nature on subsequent evenings.

Choosing Sponsors

Selecting the right sponsors for new members can be one of the most significant factors in integrating new members into the church. Having the wrong sponsors is probably worse than having none at all. Cynical, apathetic, or pushy sponsors can make people wish they had joined another congregation.

It is probably best in any church to select a relatively small group of sponsoring couples and individuals and use them again and again instead of recruiting a large number and using them infrequently. This way, more care can be exercised in the selection process, the sponsors can be trained in their work of introducing new members into congregational life, and their experience in repeated opportunities to use their training will help them to develop into new-member experts.

It is not always necessary, as it is sometimes assumed, that sponsors be of approximately the same ages and backgrounds as their sponsorees. A young person with small children often makes a very suitable sponsor for an elderly new member living in a retirement home, and sometimes a vivacious older person makes an excellent sponsor for much younger persons joining the church. The most important characteristics of a sponsor are (1) a basically friendly, likable nature and (2) an aptitude for learning from training sessions how to go about introducing new members into the life and movement of the congregation.

Meeting the Congregation

How new members are introduced to the congregation can make a big difference in the church's attitude toward assimilating new members. If the pastor handles the introduction matter-of-factly, as if it were not of any real significance, then others will probably accept the presence of strangers in their midst the same way. If he or she projects enthusiasm and happiness, on the other hand, many will feel glad to greet the new members and go out of their way to make them feel welcome.

I always introduce new members at our worship services with careful attention to their names and where they come from, and ask them to stand briefly while people turn to see and locate them. I point out that they are wearing identification tags for the morning and that they will be available in the narthex following the service for people to greet them.

Some churches with more unstructured liturgies and more time for the greeting process bring new members to the front of the congregation, where they are presented with flowers, name tags, and literature, and afterward take them to the narthex or foyer in a group, where they stand in a receiving line with the pastor or other church officers to meet the congregation. This is more difficult and time-consuming in a large congregation. But every effort should be made to provide a warm and gracious reception for those who join our churches.

The Follow-up Letter

On the Monday after people have united with our church, we send them a letter from the pastor reconfirming our joy in having them as fellow members of the body of Christ. The letter is revised from time to time, lest we ourselves begin to regard it as merely a routine communication. It usually says something like this:

Dear First Name,

It was a pleasure to receive you into our church membership yesterday. I hope you were able to feel the warmth and cordiality of our people, and to know how special it is for us to have you join us.

As we have said before, ours is a rather large congregation and it is easy to get lost from view in it. We hope you will help us to prevent this from happening in your case by availing yourself of opportunities to be a part of smaller, more vital units within the church.

As your pastor, I also hope you will not hesitate to share with me any special joys or problems you encounter along your pilgrimage in life. I shall cherish the opportunity to get to know you better.

Sincerely,

The letter is personally typed and signed. There is nothing worse, I think, than a warmly worded message reproduced on a duplicating machine and signed with a rubber stamp!

"Getting to Know ALL About You"

One of the things I soon learned in a large church is that the members are often astounded to discover, years after they first meet other members, that they have similar interests or backgrounds. I remember a man saying at a dinner party, "You went to Clemson? Dora, did you hear that? Jim went to Clemson! We're fellow alumni! By golly, I didn't know that!" Neither did Jim. They had known each other in the church for eleven years, yet neither suspected that they had attended the same institution.

It is to counter this kind of information lag and to promote networking of knowledge that we move within a few days of people's joining our congregation to obtain basic biographical data about them and publish it in our weekly newsletter. We have an official "biographer" on the staff of the newsletter, a person gifted in conversation and graciousness, who telephones or visits in people's homes and asks them engaging questions about themselves and their families, always with the warning of course that she is going to write a brief article about them.

A typical biography may read like this:

Dr. and Mrs. William H. Rumsfelt—Bill and Susan—are happy to settle in Lynchburg after several years of traveling for Uncle Sam. Bill, who received his education at the University of Georgia and Tulane Medical School, is an orthopedic surgeon, and has doctored for the U.S. Army in West Germany and at Walter Reed Hospital in Silver Spring, Md. Susan (née Deerfield), attended the University of Richmond, where she and Bill met on a blind date while he was visiting a friend. Bill enjoys hunting, woodworking, and photography, while Susan likes handicrafts, cooking, and good novels. Both are avid tennis players. They live at 2180 Trelawney Place with their three children, Bryan (age 8), Tracy Ann (age 6), and Kimberly (age 4½), plus 2 dogs, a cat, and 3 gerbils. Their letters of transfer are from the Randall Hills Baptist Church in Randall Hills, Md.

I have heard of new members receiving as many as four telephone calls from other members, following the publication of their biographies.

The Orientation Program

Orientation programs are valuable for at least three reasons: (1) they give new members something specific to become involved with during their first weeks in their new church home; (2) they are actually informative and instructive about many things new members need to know; and (3) they provide a marvelous opportunity for older members to work at the point of intersection where they can become involved in the lives and pilgrimages of the new members.

Many church orientation programs are strictly oral in nature, consisting primarly of having the pastor or someone else lecturing or teaching the new members for several Sundays prior to or following their uniting with the church. There is at least one major advantage to this. It affords maximal human contact between the pastor or pastor-surrogate and the new members. It is especially beneficial for the pastor to be able to talk directly to the people and to field their responses to whatever is said.

We rejected this method, however, in favor of a prepackaged "media" program that could be presented by rotating teams of officers without adding to the busy schedules of pastors or a sole officer. Putting the package together became the hard part of the process. What should go into it? How should it be presented?

The answer to the first question, we decided, was

[43]

fourfold and led to four separate presentations. First, we felt that most new church members needed at least a refresher course in the history of Christianity. Because we could not find a good film that depicted this history, we resorted to making a slide show of our own. Using slide photographs of great art works, we developed an illustrated lecture, with the lecture on tape, showing the rise of Christian faith following the death and resurrection of Christ, the story of Christianity in the Middle Ages and Reformation, the coming of the faith to America, and the growth of various denominations in this country.

Second, we wanted new members to know more about the history and thought of our own denomination. This was especially necessary for those coming from other denominations. Here we were fortunate in finding a good film depicting the development of Presbyterianism from John Knox to the present day.

Third, we wished to give new members an overview of the working of our own congregation. For this we produced a slide show and a narrative tape, depicting the work of our boards and mission groups; the activities of Women of the Church, Keenagers, and youth groups; the fellowship of our people; the involvement of our church in various mission activities both locally and elsewhere; the worship and study opportunities of the congregation; and many other aspects of our church's life.

Finally, we wanted something that would challenge our new members to renewed devotional life, greater commitment of self and resources, and deeper engagement in the kind of study and personal relationships necessary to continued growth in the Christian pilgrimage. For this we decided on a brief tape, to be followed by a discussion led by the officers in charge of the session.

When the four components of the program were complete, we wrote a brief guide for the officers in charge, describing step-by-step what they were to do in the presentation of the programs and suggesting questions and statements they might use in provoking meaningful discussion among the participants. The series of four programs is repeated once a quarter, with a different set of officers in charge each time. The effect on the officers is almost as salutary as that on new members themselves.

When the series was first developed, we showed parts of it to officers' groups and used the segment on the history of the faith as a program for a fellowship dinner. The response was so positive that word got around quickly, and now the series is rarely given without a number of older church members, including a Sunday school class or two, present to enjoy it.

"A Tea in Your Honor"

We always attempt, when making announcements and acknowledging visitors at fellowship dinners, to focus on members who have recently joined. It is often a pleasure to find that some of them are on the serving staff for the dinner, having already been recruited by the Fellowship Mission Group.

I hope, though, we can soon go a step farther by having some special event to honor our new members, such as a quarterly tea on a Sunday afternoon or a breakfast on a Sunday morning. The tea could be a simple affair, with tea and coffee and cookies, candlelight, and a few flowers. Officers would be urged to be present, and the entire congregation would be invited. People could chat in small clusters, with the officers and pastors moving around from group to group. Then there might be a brief statement about our delight in honoring our recently acquired friends, followed by a short introduction of each of them, made by various officers. This might be followed by some words of encouragement about getting involved in the work of the church. After a bit more visiting, people could simply drift away when they feel it is time to go.

Again, as at the meeting when they first met with the Session, people would be provided with name tags for ease in making introductions and calling one another's names.

[45]

The Six-Month Checkup

As I mentioned earlier, our church now uses Friendship Books to track the attendance of both visitors and members. When a member has missed five consecutive Sundays, the MIA committee* of our Pastoral Mission Group swings into action with a telephone call or visit to say, "Hey, we've been missing you at church. Hope nothing's wrong." The Friendship Books are especially helpful in checking up on new members to be sure they haven't joined the membership and dropped out of sight.

But we also like to make a special checkup on new members after they have been in the church for six months to see how well they have become assimilated into our work and fellowship. To this end, we have developed a Six-Month Checkup questionnaire. The Pastoral Mission Group receives a monthly list of persons who have been members of the church for six months, and these persons are visited or called by someone responsible for completing the questionnaire and returning it to the Mission Group.

Here is the checkup form used by the member of the Pastoral Mission Group:

SIX-MONTH CHECKUP ON NEW MEMBERS

Suggested Introduction

Hello, this is _____. I'm calling for the Pastoral Mission Group of First Presbyterian Church. We like to get in touch with all our new members after they've been in the church for six months and see how well they are settling in their new church home. Do you mind if I ask you a few brief questions?

---

*For "Missing in Action." We used this name because we couldn't think of another when we were forming the Pastoral Mission Group, and it stuck.

The Care and Feeding of New Members

The Questions

(Please make brief but intelligible notes of all answers and return them to the Pastoral Mission Group. Answers may be noted on this sheet.)

Do you attend a church school class on a regular basis?

Have you joined the choir or any other organization of the church?

Have you attended any fellowship dinners?

Do you have children? Are they involved in youth activities of the church?

Have you used the church library since joining the church?

Have you been visited by anyone from the church?

Did you attend the orientation program for new members?

Do you know about Hearthsiders, our rotation dinner program?

Have you attended any seminars in the church since joining?

Have you made a stewardship commitment since joining?

Do you still enjoy the worship services of the church?

Have you completed and returned the Commitment Form you were given when you joined the church?

Have you been called on to perform any service in the church?

Have you attended any special services such as Ash Wednesday, Maundy Thursday, Thanksgiving Day, or Christmas Eve?

Have you become involved with any church-related service organizations?

Do you have any suggestions to offer for the consideration of our pastors or officers?

Well, that completes our questionnaire. I've enjoyed our little visit and I appreciate your giving me this time. We want you to become as integral a part of the church as possible, and hope you won't hesitate to call the pastors if there is anything they can do to help you. Thank you very much.

When the checkup forms are returned to the Pastoral Mission Group they are studied for patterns of assimilation or non-assimilation. If they show patterns of non-assimilation they are turned over to the pastors, who schedule a visit with the members to try to help them toward a more disciplined plan of involvement in the church.

The retention and training of new members is essential to the future life of the church. When I look over our membership now and think of several of the more vital, attractive, and aggressive members who have joined our fellowship in the last three or four years, I realize what we would be missing if they had dropped out in the early months of their pilgrimage with us. Then I try to imagine what we have missed in the persons who did drop out, who, for one reason or another, failed to mesh and become involved in the life of our congregation. A sense of sadness and regret crosses my mind as if the shadow of a cloud had passed over it. If we had only done a better job of pastoring, they might be vitally engaged now, fulfilling their own needs as individuals and helping us all fulfill our commitment as the church of Jesus Christ!

III

Making Children Feel at Home

"Suffer the little children to come unto me, and forbid them not," said Jesus, "for of such is the kingdom of God" (Mark 10:14 KJV). In some churches, you sure wouldn't know it. I didn't know it in the church I attended as a child. Children there were shushed and shunned, and treated as though we were necessary evils in the lives of adults who wanted to visit one another and worship God without any interference from us. I was a timid child, moreover, and didn't feel that I belonged with the other children. Church was a bad scene for me. It wasn't until I was a teenager and found another church, where children were not only welcome but considered special, that I began to think of God as something more than a Cosmic Frown and an Almighty Giver of Measles and Stomachaches!

In most churches today, of course, there are conflicting ideologies about children. On one hand, parents spoil children as they were never spoiled before. They give them everything—TV sets, computers, mud-bikes, electric guitars, dolls that cry and talk and wet and grow hair. They tolerate behavior that was not tolerated by their own parents—bad manners, tantrums, foul language, messiness, rebellion. And they take a greater interest in their children than the parents of any previous generation, often literally agonizing over their growth and development. But, on the other hand, they often neglect their spiritual training and, when it comes to worship, usually they prefer to have the children cared for elsewhere so that they can sit in peace and comfort. Worship services, as a result, are frequently segregated affairs, with everything being done for adults and almost nothing done for children and young people. "That is what we hire youth workers for," said one woman, as though having caretakers for the children abrogated all her responsibilities for their spiritual upbringing.

Children, just as adults, need to be integrated into the planning, work, and worship of the church. The character of the integration may be debatable; I can never forget Albert Schweitzer's statement that he was glad no accommodations were made to children in the worship services he attended as a child, for in those services he first became aware of the tremendous awe and mystery of God. But the fact of integration is not debatable. Those of us who have influence over the nature of the church's work and worship should expend every effort to be inclusive of children and to make them feel at home with the journey of faith.

Ring Around the Font

Our church practices infant baptism. Even though I was once a minister of a denomination that baptized only "believers," or persons old enough to make their own decisions for Christ, I have had no problem with the theology of baptizing babies and infants. One problem I have had with the practical side of infant baptism, however, is that many parents do not instruct their children about their baptism, even though they promised to do so. As a result the children grow to adulthood without a very real impression or understanding of their baptism.

To counter this tendency in our church, all the children in the congregation are invited to gather around the font at the time of a baptism so that they have front-row seats and can see what is done. As I carry the child who has been baptized into the chancel for the choir and congregation to get a better view of him or her, I often pause among the children to make a comment such as, "Do you remember when you were this small and were baptized?" or "Do you think this beautiful little baby will remember this when she is as old as you?" This way, I hope to reinforce again and again the "memory" of their own baptism and provoke discussion of the subject in their families.

In all my years of doing this, I have never seen a child misbehave either in front of the congregation or while leaving or returning to parents. There is a raptness on the children's faces through the entire ritual, as if they realize they are witnessing something both special and holy. Their presence around the font makes baptism doubly meaningful to me.

Deepening the Experience of Baptism

Our baptisms are included in the usual Sunday morning liturgy as part of the flow of congregational worship. This underlines our particular theology of baptism, that it is a congregational act and not a private act limited to the minister, the infant, and the parents. But, as this imposes on us the possibility that the baptismal rite will become tedious, we have developed four or five alternate rites and shift them about from Sunday to Sunday. In each one, there are parts for the congregation and assisting elders as well as for the minister and the parents.

Not long ago, it struck me that baptismal moments in worship might be further enhanced if we had some special chorus or blessing the choir could sing as part of the ritual. When I couldn't find an appropriate resonse for the occasion, I wrote down a few words and my wife graciously set them to music. We now use the following blessing at each baptism, while the children are returning to their parents, and welcome anyone else to use it.

As part of our effort to make baptism more meaningful, we also present the parents with a gift-wrapped edition of

BAPTISMAL BLESSING

Words by John Killinger

Music by Anne Killinger

John Westerhoff's little book *Will Our Children Have Faith?* And we are contemplating the practice of having a photographer make a picture of the parents and child with the minister and elders after the service, so that the portrait will be a visible reminder of the baptism when the child is older.

Acolytes

The word *acolyte* is derived from the Greek *akolouthos*, which means "follower." It was originally applied to priests who assisted at Mass, and, later, in the Anglican Church, to laymen who had similar duties. Eventually it came to designate an altar boy, and finally, in the contemporary church, a boy or girl who lights the candles in the chancel or performs some other duty in the proximity of the altar or communion table.

Our Worship Mission Group decided to institute the use of acolytes in our services in order to give children a more focal place in the worship of God. The Children's Choir did sing once a month at the early service, but otherwise children were visible only in the pews, with their parents. We wanted to give them something to do that would be more inspiring and dramatic for them.

A member of the congregation volunteered to train the children, arrange their schedules, see that they are robed, and dispatch them from the rear of the nave at precisely the right moment in each service. The children's names are printed in the bulletin each week—two for each service—and they appear punctually, lighting the altar candles at the conclusion of the prelude and the time for the introit. When the choir has recessed at the end of the service, they proceed again to the chancel and extinguish the candles, then stand attentively at the sides of the altar until the benediction is said or sung.

Everyone in the sanctuary feels a thrill at watching the children approach the chancel. They have such intent looks on their faces, inspired partly, no doubt, by fears that the light on the taper may go out in the movement. But there is something angelic about them in the performance of this sacred duty—something that will affect them and their feelings about worship for the remainder of their lives. I only wish we could employ ten instead of two of them at every service!

Youthful Ushers

Another revision we have made to include more children in our worship is to ask families to receive the offering at one morning service. As only four persons are required for this duty, we normally have two parents and two children. But occasionally, if one of the children is very small, there will be three children and one of the parents will merely oversee the smallest child.

It would be hard to describe the beaming faces of the children as they stand before the communion table for the offertory prayer, or the equally happy looks on the faces of adults as the children make their way up the aisles, handling the offering plates. The entire exchange is nothing short of sacramental.

And when the doxology is sung and the entire family strides down the aisle with the offering, the children leading the way—well, God must be more pleased with our offerings then than when they are borne by mere adults!

Worship Workshop

Some marvelous women in our church decided that it isn't enough to include children in worship and involve

them in the actions of the liturgy, that they ought also to be trained in the meaning of worship. So they undertook, with the help of a staff adviser and some literature, to inaugurate and maintain a weekly worship workshop for preschool and early school-age children. The workshop takes the place of what many churches observe as Junior Church or Children's Worship. Children remain in the regular worship service until after the doxology, or just before the sermon, and then they retire from the sanctuary to a chapel where the themes of morning worship are continued, but with instruction as part of the format.

The only exception to this is on Communion Sunday, the first Sunday of each month, when the children remain in the sanctuary through the entire service.

In the Worship Workshop, they learn the meaning of the Lord's Prayer and the Apostles' Creed, learn to sing the "Gloria Patri," the doxology, and a few frequently used hymns, and receive instruction in the various symbols and actions of worship. They are also led to an understanding of baptism and the Lord's Supper and of how to listen to the Bible readings and the sermon.

The Worship Workshop leaders prepare special bulletins and place them on tables for the children and their parents to pick up as they enter the sanctuary each Sunday. Coordinated with the orders of worship for the day, these bulletins contain word and picture exercises for the children to consider and work on during the liturgy. They may say, for example, "What did the minister do when he said during the baptism, 'I now baptize you in the name of the Father and the Son and the Holy Ghost'? You may draw a picture of it if you wish." Parents are encouraged to quietly assist the children in understanding questions or instructions they cannot grasp alone.

I have seen, in the two years we have had Worship Workshop, a marvelous sharpening of our children's comprehension of what is occurring during worship.

Sometimes I think they understand better than many of their parents. I have also seen some fantastic drawings made during the services, one of which, drawn by eight-year-old Kina Gimbert, is reproduced on page 54.

Blessing the Animals

One of our members, who participated in a Blessing of the Animals Service in Florida, approached our director of Christian education and together they approached me about having such a service in our church. We looked at the calendar. In October, the church universal would be celebrating the five-hundredth anniversary of the birth of St. Francis. Why not? It would be the perfect occasion! So we set about the planning, and on a beautifully clear Sunday afternoon in October, 1982, we gathered on the church lawn to celebrate God's gift of animals and share our sense of blessing with the family pets.

There was a large crowd. The lawn was well covered with both people and animals. There were dogs, cats, gerbils, hamsters, mice, goldfish, parakeets, canaries, and even a couple of snakes. And there were photographers galore, including a local TV crew. There were pastors in robes, a portable lectern with built-in amplifier, printed bulletins, and music from guests with guitars and ballads.

The liturgy included the reading of Genesis 1:20-28, the story of the creation of birds, fish, animals, and human beings; litanies about animals, nature, and ecology; the singing of "All Creatures Great and Small"; and a homily based on Isaiah's vision of the kingdom of God:

The wolf shall dwell with the lamb,
and the leopard shall lie down with the kid,
and the calf and the lion and the fatling
together,
and a little child shall lead them.
The cow and the bear shall feed;

their young shall lie down together;
and the lion shall eat straw like the ox.

(Isa. 11:6-7)

The actual blessing of the animals, which I accomplished by passing among the crowd and laying my hands on the animals (I touched only the containers of the birds, fish, and snakes!) was done while our musicians sang a song about God and the animals.

It was a gala occasion. The children loved it and the adults loved it. The pets, I fear, were largely indifferent, aside from the aggression triggered in some of the dogs when they saw one another. But the children talked about it for weeks and began eagerly to look forward to another service of blessing the next year.

Special Gestures

If and when I leave my present parish, it will be the children I will miss the most. Every pastor knows how special they are. From the time you hold them in your arms for a baptism until they go away to college, they are *your* children. They wave to you from fast-moving cars, run up to you in the corridors of the church, bring you crazy little gifts or homemade Valentines, and generally introduce large quantities of sunshine into your life. It is easy to love them and easy to do special things for them.

I always try to make over them when they come through the reception line on Sunday morning, noticing their new clothes, their haircuts, their missing teeth, their new bruises and breaks, and especially their growth since the last time I saw them. One little fellow who hardly speaks always comes up shyly for his lift and hug and occasionally tells me secrets. Little twin girls love to tease me about their identities; I have even accused them of going off and changing dresses to fool me again on the same day. I want to run away with all of them.

Often I write one of my little friends a letter, especially if he or she has done something nice for me, such as given

[57]

me a handmade lei or a greeting card or a cookie. I will say something like:

Dear Katie,
   It was awfully sweet of you to give me the drawing you made of our church. I think it looks very much like the church, don't you? I have put it under the lamp on my desk so I will see it every morning this week when I come to work. I think of you each time I look at it. Thank you for making it for me.

I love you,
Dr. John

To this day, I remember the kindness shown to me by a local minister when I was a boy of five or six, and I suspect that these little citizens of the kingdom will one day recall that a minister loved them too.

The real sweetheart of our congregation is little Sarah Margaret, a Downs syndrome child who was born into our church family in the summer of 1981. When Sarah Margaret's parents spoke to me about her baptism, I knew what they had been through in learning to accept her condition and that having her baptized was not an easy step for them to take. People in the community had never been very open about Downs children. "Would you be willing," I asked them, "to have the whole service built around Sarah Margaret?" They thought about the question for a few days and responded positively.

The entire liturgy focused on Sarah Margaret's baptism. The following Affirmation of Faith was used:

I believe in the God of little children
   who creates them warm and tender
      in their mothers' wombs
   and bestows them as gifts
   millions of times each year
   upon both rich and poor.
I believe in Jesus Christ,
   who said, "Suffer the little children
      to come unto me,"
   and in the kingdom he said would be comprised
   entirely of childlike beings.

[58]

Making Children Feel at Home

I believe in the Holy Spirit of God
  that broods over the face of the deep,
    claiming this child and that
  for the service of God in all humanity
  through art and music, science and industry,
    government and church, and
      a thousand other ways.
It is a rich world, alive with the potential
    of all its children
  waiting to transform our lives
  for the glory of Father, Son, and Holy Spirit.
  Amen.

The anthem was a haunting ballad titled "He Was a Lamb." It was about a lamb born into a world of wolves, and the way he grew into a handsome, rugged sheep before the wolves finally killed him. But then, after his hide was hung on a tree, he rose from the dead, and lives today.

The confession of sin, which followed immediately after the anthem, asked forgiveness for our having been wolves instead of lambs, and having neglected the lambs of the world.

The meditation was entitled "A Sermon for Sarah," and spoke frankly of Sarah Margaret's handicap and of the pain her parents would feel many times in her life. But it also pointed to the joy she would be to all of us and to the sense of grace she would bring among us.

After her baptism, the congregation joined together in making this promise:

Dear Sarah:
Though you will not understand this now, we are involved with you in a very special way. We are, all together, children of the covenant. As we ourselves were once baptized, now we stand to welcome your baptism. It is the way we are brought into the household of faith. As your brothers and sisters in this household, we greet your arrival with love and rejoicing. We covet for you a life filled with all good things of Spirit and pledge ourselves to helping make that possible. We wish you to live continually in the presence of Christ, and so shall dedicate

ourselves to him anew, that you may experience him through us. May God hold you gently and love you strongly is our prayer in Jesus' name. Amen.

Sarah Margaret has become, as I said, the sweetheart of our congregation. The service helped carve a special place in our lives for her. Eveyone watches over her. When she first began walking, crowds of people applauded her. Her father has been elected a deacon, and her mother teaches a circle in Women of the Church. Their faith and devotion have become examples to everybody in the congregation. And several older couples who had had Downs babies and had secretly institutionalized them began to speak openly of their children and deal with their guilt and hurt.

Making Confirmation Special

In churches that practice infant baptism and confirmation of young persons in the faith, confirmation is one of the most important processes for both pastors and young people. Few rituals require as much planning, imagination, and thoughtful shepherding. Successfully training and guiding young people through this event can bind them to the church for life; dealing with it unsuccessfully can lose them for life.

It is a multiple event in which relationships and psychological growth play as important a role as doctrinal understanding and intellectual stimulation. Something warm and good and wholesome needs to happen to the group and the individuals within it. One hesitates to use the word conversion too easily, and yet that is precisely what must take place. The participants are led through one stage of their life's conversion to Christ. There will be other stages later—when they become drivers and voters, when they enter the work force, when they marry, when they have children, when they reach mid-life, when they retire. But no stage is more significant than this one. If it is not negotiated successfully, there may not be other conversions to come.

Our confirmation classes, because of the exigencies and pressures of children's lives during the school week, have become Saturday affairs, stretching over half a dozen Saturdays during Lent. They are taught by the very best teachers we can get—pastors, a professor of religion from a local college, and some devoted instructors from within the congregation. Not enough of the instruction is done with exciting media, I fear; I am hopeful that some imaginative film makers will come up with some usefully packaged materials for confirmation classes. But every care is taken to see that the material we use is fresh, that the teaching methods are first-rate, and that the experience is a positive one for the youngsters involved.

In the course of the confirmation sessions, each child is assigned to an officer of the church. Officers are encouraged to use their own resourcefulness in planning special dinners, outings, or other affairs with their assignees during the period. Then, on the final Saturday of the series, we have an officer-child breakfast at which the young people are honored and examined before being voted on for confirmation by the elders.

(I have heard of churches where the climax of the confirmation classes is a retreat involving pastors, officers, and young people, with the adults joining the youngsters for skiing, bobsledding, volleyball, or other "fun" activities, and I admit that this sounds even better than what we do!)

With our last confirmation class, we followed a trend in many churches of holding an Easter-Eve Baptism and Confirmation Service, and found it very impressive and exciting. All the candidates for baptism and confirmation wore white and sat in the front of the sanctuary, with friends and parents behind them. We had a full-blown liturgy, with prayers, readings, presentation of candidates, declaration of repentance and commitment, recital of the Apostles' Creed, baptism of those who had not been baptized as infants, a sermon-meditation, and Communion. The service, with some amendments, was essentially that of *A Service of Baptism, Confirmation, and Renewal, The United Methodist Church, an Alternate Text 1976*.

Few services in our church have ever been more meaningful. "I wouldn't have been surprised," said one starry-eyed youngster being confirmed, "if I had looked up and seen Jesus Christ standing in the choir stalls!"

"It was beautiful," said the grandfather of one of the children. "If I had had a service like that when I was confirmed forty-four years ago, my life would have been better than it has been."

"Congratulations, Graduate!"

One of the principles of good pastoring has always been to weep with those who are weeping and rejoice with those who are rejoicing. There is no time when this principle is truer than in the late spring when many young people and their families are caught up in graduation fever. It is the final opportunity we have as a church to recognize and celebrate events in the lives of some of our young people, who will be going off to college or work perhaps never to be a part of our lives again. We have chosen in our congregation, therefore, to make Graduation Sunday an event of real importance.

First, we send letters to all the graduates extolling them for their accomplishments and inviting them to be present for a special service. They gather on Sunday in the narthex, wearing their robes of graduation, and follow the choir to reserved seats in the front of the sanctuary. Two of them read the scripture lessons for the day. The prayers and remarks are designed to include references to the graduates and their families, and the sermon is directed especially to the graduates. They are individually acknowledged and presented with gift books signed by the pastor. In short, every effort is made to make them feel that their church cares about them and their plans for the future.

Here is a copy of the prayer that adorned the front of the bulletin for one of these services:

Grant to our sons and daughters, O Lord, a vision of life that is whole and pure. Let them see themselves in the perspective of the ages, that they may take themselves seriously but not too seriously, that they may plan for the future, and that they may avoid the pitfalls so common to our flesh. Give them excitement for the world they are discovering, joy in their relationships, and satisfaction in their work. Bestow upon them the blessing of meaningful involvement in the pain and growth of their greater environment. And finally, O Lord, let them enter your heavenly kingdom to the words, "Well done, thou good and faithful servant," that they may live with you forever and ever. Amen.

And here is an Affirmation of Faith written especially for a graduation service:

We believe in the God of children, who ordains his truths to come from the mouths of babes and receives them into his heavenly kingdom;

We believe in the God of young people, who guides them in the course of their development and calls them into his eternal service;

We believe in the God of young adults, who blesses them with work for their hands and hope for the world they are building;

We believe in the God of older adults, who forgives their shortcomings, hears their prayers for the young, and helps them see the beauty of all their relationships.

We believe in the God of the elderly, who prepares them even in this life for the blessedness of the life to come, and whispers in their sleep of the wholeness that awaits them beyond;

We believe in the God of all ages, who himself is ageless but walks with us in every age; it is he who has made us and not we ourselves; and he will be with us as the shepherd of the sheep, ever leading us into green pastures, through Christ his Son and the Holy Spirit, to whom be glory forever and ever. Amen.

We try to follow our young people to college and into military service, writing to them and inviting them to keep in touch with us. But we always feel satisfied about pulling out all the stops for the Graduation Service. It our way of pronouncing a benediction on our children as they leave us to go out into the world.

IV

Shepherding Older Members

One imagines that Christianity in its early years was a youth movement, fueled by young men and women ready to go beyond the traditions of their elders. Today, in many churches, it appears to be exactly the opposite—a society of elderly people gathered to sing the old hymns and remember when the faith was young and vital. Not that the elderly are more devoted to the past or the status quo than younger people. On the contrary, they are often among the freest folks in a congregation, having outgrown the pressures of their productive years and outlived the time when they had to conform to social patterns.

Our church is fortunate to have a healthy spectrum of age representation, with many young people to bring fire and vision to its ministry and many older people to bring love and joy and gentleness. But it is the older people who most often warm the pastor's heart. As I confessed in a "Pastor's Paragraph" early on in my present ministry, I am really "an old-folks junkie." Their accumulation of experience, their way of looking at the world, their self-mocking sense of humor frequently keep me going on days when I want to stop. Anybody who thinks pastors spend a lot of time with the elderly because they have to is only half-right; we also do it because we like to! Shepherding older members is a lot of fun. They return the shepherding.

Celebrating Birthdays

People in mid-life often like to forget their birthdays; they don't like the thought of growing older. But older people seem to enjoy their birthdays almost as much as they did when they were children. They like parties and cakes and cards and other remembrances as symbols of love and fellowship—and perhaps as symbols of congratulations that they have survived another year!

The birthdays of all our older folks are among the items we try to record in our Book of Days, so that a special phone call, a card, or a visit from the pastor will be one of their birthday remembrances. If the person is over ninety, we make it a rule to note the birthday in our newsletter and perhaps even in the church bulletin. Somehow, when people get that old, they become special to everyone, not just to those who know them well. Between ninety-five and one hundred, we really pull out all the stops.

For example, at our last February fellowship dinner, which was held on Valentine's Day, we had a musical program featuring a popular singer in our church. Midway in the program, the singer stopped to wish a particularly happy Valentine's Day to Mrs. Bess Younger, who was ninety-nine years old. Bess does not usually attend fellowship dinners, though she still comes to many Women of the Church functions. But special care had been taken to see that she got to this one and that she wore a bright red dress which had been in her closet for years. That evening, as she sat near the front of the hall, our entertainer drew the spotlight to her and announced that she was our "Sweetheart of the Year." A gentleman who had also sung a couple of songs that evening appeared at her side with a bouquet of roses and sang "Let Me Call You Sweetheart." Bess was delighted, as everyone was. She deserved the attention. Ninety-nine is no mean accomplishment!

Neither is a hundred. A few months earlier, one of our members, Mrs. Fannie Moore, celebrated her one-hundredth birthday. Our church had never had a homecoming, so we planned one to coincide with Fannie's birthday. Two former ministers of the church came back to preach. The choir sang Fannie's favorite anthems. We had the largest dinner in the church hall that was ever held there. A local baker donated a birthday cake for every table and a large one for Fannie's table. A restaurateur donated gallons and gallons of ice cream. We sang "Happy Birthday" and paid oral tributes to Fannie. In the course of this, Fannie asked for the microphone and told a humorous tale from her past. With money left over from the fund for the celebration, we commissioned a water colorist to make a large portrait of the church, and had it framed with a small plaque under it honoring Fannie.

It was a great occasion for Fannie, but an even greater one in the life of our congregation. Our spirits soared for weeks afterward!

Interviews and Biographies

The elderly may complain that modern society is no longer interested in their views or lives, but that complaint ought never to be heard in the church. The past is one of our greatest treasures, and the memories of our older folk are the crown jewels of that treasure.

Another way we honor the elderly is by interviewing them and putting their opinions and biographies in our newsletter. We believe it is important for our young people to know something about living history and to realize, when they see Aunt Dinah or Grandpa Brown in the corridors of the church, that they are repositories of faith and experience whom we genuinely value. The elderly, of course, are usually delighted by the attention.

I mentioned earlier Mrs. Bess Younger, whose ninety-ninth year was acknowledged at our Valentine dinner. Here is the brief tribute to her that appeared in our newsletter for April 2, 1981, shortly before her ninety-sixth birthday:

Shepherding Older Members

Younger Is Older—In Years Only!

Bessie Mason Younger, affectionately known as Bess, will celebrate her 96th birthday on April 4th. She was born in Campbell County, and came to Lynchburg as the bride of Dr. Edward F. Younger. From that marriage, she has a very devoted stepson, E. Franklin Younger, who is a retired lawyer in Lynchburg. She has several nieces and nephews, but one niece, Maude Younger, lives in Lynchburg and has been a great help to her since her surgery.

Bess had a leg amputated in January 1980 and was fitted for an artificial limb. Now she gets around better than most of us. While she was recuperating at home after the surgery, a bridge group was formed to keep her occupied. Hilda Gentry, Anne Hammerstrom, and Lois Sales met with her on a regular basis, and, in fact, still do. Hilda says that Bess keeps them straight when the other three can't remember who bid what!

This lovely lady is an inspiration to everyone. She's beautiful, always looks radiant, is independent, loves to cook, and still makes homemade bread. She is a treat to be around.

In the past Bess has been very active in Sunday school and W.O.C., where she was a circle chairman, and always attended church regularly. She is a member of the D.A.R. and U.D.C. (United Daughters of the Confederacy). If you don't see her at church very often, it is because she has a bit of a hearing problem and worships with us every week by radio.

Hilda Gentry tells this story:

After Bess had surgery, Hilda was to pick her up for Sunday school and church. Thinking she would need plenty of time to get Bess down the stairs and into the car, Hilda allowed an extra twenty minutes. She parked her car and went up the stairs. There was Bess standing in the doorway with pocketbook and cane in hand. When Hilda offered to assist her in the descent, Bess said, "You just take my pocketbook and cane and go on down." Bess walked down alone, took her belongings, and seated herself in the car. The whole process took three minutes.

Now you understand why she's considered an inspiration by everyone who knows her. We hope she has a glorious 96th, and our birthday wish is for many more to follow!

A big picture of a birthday cake accompanied the article.

[67]

The Tender Shepherd

A Radio Program for Shut-Ins

This is the age of TV, and our church is located in a city that has helped make TV religion part of the modern spectacle. Our own role in media is much more modest. We broadcast our eleven o'clock Sunday morning worship service for the sake of our elderly folks and those who happen to be ill or away for the weekend at a nearby lake or mountain home. And the broadcast is live, as opposed to recorded, in order that they may feel a participating role in the worship. The order of worship, complete with hymns, is published in the newsletter each week, and many of our shut-ins, who have hymnbooks at home, sit with their order of worship and follow the entire service with us, some even to the point of singing. I usually mention them in the words of welcome and often include them in the pastoral or corporate prayer. For them, radio is still a more important medium for religion than TV.

The investment in such broadcasting is very modest, and well worth it as a service that includes all of our elderly people in the weekly worship of God. They appreciate it and see it as an expression of the church's care for them. As one elderly woman put it, "I don't need a TV set when I can use the radio. I always could 'see' more on radio anyway, when the programs were good. And I can see everything that's happening in my church!"

Cassettes and Casseroles

In addition to regularly broadcasting our worship services, we try to tape-record them and make them available on cassettes to our older folks or anyone else who wants them. Some of our elderly people like to listen to them over and over through the week, lingering over the hymns and almost memorizing the prayers. I am always amazed at some dear woman in her eighties who says, "Remember when you prayed, 'O Lord, make us grateful for small inconveniences that remind us of large opportunities,'" and I can't recall it at all, despite her assurances that it was on one of the worship tapes. In this way the tape recording extends the ministry of the worship hour.

Even more important for our shut-ins is the tape recording of seminars, musical events, and programs that go on at the church but are not broadcast. By making copies of these available to our people who cannot be at the church, we include them in the activities and fellowship in a way that would otherwise be denied them.

It is a particular delight, the day after a special program at a fellowship dinner or the preaching of some famous guest in our annual preaching mission, to be able to take a tape and a cassette player to someone at home or in the hospital and say, "Here is what went on at church last night; we want you to be a part of it too."

Our Women of the Church group prepares and freezes casserole dishes so they will be available for persons just returning home from a stay in the hospital. Sometimes, when we take a tape of a special event to a shut-in, we take along a casserole too. "Now," we say, "you can eat and listen at the same time."

The sermons preached in our pulpit are also printed in brochure-sized foldouts handy for slipping in a man's coat pocket or a woman's purse. These are available each week in a literature rack in the narthex, and many of our worshipers pick up copies to take to shut-ins and friends in retirement homes. Older people have more time to read than they once did, and they genuinely appreciate having their own church's printed materials to pore over at odd hours of the day or evening. Our sermons, I explain, are like radioactive materials; they have a strong half-life that continues to work after they have been preached!

Regular Visits from the Pastors

Most of us who are fit and able to circulate in the community seldom think of the plight of many older persons who have become basically immobile and experience life primarily as it is brought to them by visitors. I think, for example, of one of the finest women in our church, who spent much of her time until she was past eighty visiting the sick, running errands for the elderly, and entertaining people in her home. After a series of debilitating illnesses and injuries, including a broken hip, she became confined to her bedroom in the large old house where her family had been raised. Her only view of the world was seen from an upstairs window. She sat by the window most of the day, watching for people to come to see her. They were her primary contacts with the outside world where she had once been so happily occupied.

Visits by the pastors are extremely important to such persons. The pastors represent the church that has long been so dear to them. And the pastors are able to relay news of other people in the parish, especially the old friends these people would most like to see. I have never visited the lady I mentioned above without having her ask, "Oh, tell me about so-and-so, how is she getting along?" or "Tell me about dear Mr. So-and-So. Is he feeling any better these days?"

Young pastors sometimes appear to regret that caring for the elderly is one of their pastoral duties, as though this were not part of the kingdom's work they bargained for. But I have always found my visits with older folks to be one of the most rewarding aspects of all my pastoral work. They are much freer of life's burdens and restraints than younger people and are often quite refreshing in their openness and candor. And their perspectives on life are usually much saner than those of persons still caught up in the business of making a living and rearing children.

I remember Miss Eva Moore, whom we pastors visited regularly until her death a few months ago. Miss Eva, who was in her nineties, received an M.A. degree from Columbia University seventy years ago, when such an education was uncommon for women, and taught school until her retirement. Her Victorian-style house was filled with books—mostly classics—and she was still reading them shortly before her death. When I called on her, we sat among the books and talked of Chaucer and Shakespeare and Dickens, and of how inadequate many of the TV productions are in comparison with these great authors. Then we spoke of current events, and Miss Eva always commented on them from the point of view of history and her long experience. I came away feeling refreshed for the day, as though after a long hike through the hot desert I had spent an hour sitting by the cool spray from a waterfall.

And of course Miss Eva and I always talked about religion. She told me about the many spiritual experiences of her long lifetime, and we discussed passages from the Bible. Older people often have insights into religious truth that pastors need to hear. They are like gyroscopes, returning us to levels of sanity and relevance in our thinking. I always felt more balanced and whole after a visit with Miss Eva.

In our church, we keep lists of all our shut-ins and retirees, and our Pastoral Mission Group sees that they are visited regularly by lay visitors. But the pastors try to see these persons on a routine basis too. We even visit the ones who have become senile and no longer appear to recognize us. Who knows but that somewhere, deep in the recesses of the brain, they experience a glint of recognition and the pastor becomes a vital link between this world and the one to which they travel.

Communion on Demand

The first year I was in my present parish, we took communion to all the shut-ins in the church, with the exception of two or three who, when we phoned ahead, said they preferred not to have it. Afterward, when we assessed the effects of this, we realized that while some of the people were genuinely happy to receive the sacrament in their homes there were others who regarded it either as an invasion of privacy or as a sign that we believed they were getting ready to die. In subsequent years, therefore, we have made a practice of asking through the newsletter and bulletin for the names of persons who would like us to bring communion into their homes. We call on all of our shut-ins during the special seasons, such as Christmas and Easter, and take communion to those who desire it.

When we do make a call with communion, we begin amiably, as in any visit, with talk of the weather, the shut-in's health, the family, and so on. Then we say, "We are glad you wanted to join us in a celebration of the Lord's Meal," and go on to talk briefly about the significance of the meal. We read some scriptures, including the words of institution, have a prayer, and share the elements. Then we have another prayer, thank the shut-ins for having us, and retire.

One of the discoveries I have made is the importance of taking an elderly person along to assist in these "services." In our church, the Book of Order specifies that another elder should be present with the pastor, and I often try to get an elder who has been retired from active service and is delighted for the opportunity of assisting in this manner. If this elder is of the same generation as the person being visited, they have a wonderful opportunity to talk about friends they have in common, to reminisce about old times, and to comfort each other in the latter days of their life's journeys.

One such elder commented to me as we were leaving a home where we had served communion, "This means more to me now than it ever did in all the years I served communion in the church!"

The Special Opportunity of Retirement Homes

Retirement homes present a special opportunity for pastoral service. We have a wonderful Westminster-Canterbury center only half a mile from our church, and many of our older members are living there. We can do more pastoring there in an hour than we can get done in other parts of the city in a day. A stroll through the commons area produces five of six spontaneous visits with old friends and often turns up pastoral needs either in their lives or the lives of friends. A meal taken in the refectory affords dozens of greetings and a chance to visit in some depth with three or four persons around the table. And giving the meditation or offering communion in chapel puts us in contact with all of our residents plus dozens of their friends and associates.

With the exception of our regular services of worship in the church, I know of no more important or economical use of our time and energies than the leadership of chapel at Westminster-Canterbury. It not only allows us to minister to many of our members at the same time, but permits us to do it with a kind of concentration that is impossible even in the church. That is, because all the attendants at worship in the retirement center are in the same age group, the hymns, prayers, readings, and meditations can be focused much more effectively than when we are dealing with a wider spectrum of members, as we must in the church.

I have found that our folks at Westminster-Canterbury respond quite positively to more whimsical or imaginative kinds of programs and chapel talks as well as to traditional kinds. Perhaps it is due to the setting, which is not quite that of the church, even though it is reverent and spiritual in nature. So I often let my mind range a little more freely in preparing for a service there, and they are always responsive. Here, for example, are some semi-humorous prayers I have used as a collection of meditations on age and its problems:

> Those were great creampuffs
> we had for dinner, Lord.
> Only I'm afraid
> they had about three thousand
> calories in them.
> My fat cells just reached out
> and embraced them.
> Not a one got away.
> Now they are all nestled
> around my middle,
> where everything seems

to congregate these days.
Were there any calories
in the Garden of Eden, Lord?
Surely there won't be any in heaven.
It would be hell
if there were.

I declare, Lord,
I must be growing
a lot of hair
these days,
because
there is always
more on my brush
than on my head
when I finish
grooming it!

I had a long distance call
today, Lord.
It was from my son in California.
The ads are right, Lord,
it was almost as good
as having him here.
I hope there'll be telephones
in heaven, Lord.
I'll miss them
if there aren't.

The people chuckled, and afterward assured me that
they understood all the allusions. "One of the beautiful
things about growing older," said one old fellow, "is that
you no longer have to change things or make the world
over. All you have to do is recognize them and thank God
for having let you live."

Won't You Be My Valentine?

Valentines are for kids, right? Wrong! They often
mean more to adults than they do to youngsters.
Especially older adults. My wife, who is an old-folks
junkie too, always remembers this at Valentine's Day
and purchases large, beautiful cards to send to the eight

or ten oldest members of our congregation. It is a colorful way of saying, "We love you, have a happy day!"

I don't know of anything that produces a greater effect in our relationship with these people.

Last year, one of these women wrote us a note. In trembling hand, she said: "It was the nicest thing. It made my whole day when I opened it. I set it on the mantel and look at it every time I pass. 'That's from my pastor and his wife,' I think. I'm so grateful."

When another woman fell and broke her hip, I called on her in the hospital. "Oh," she said, "I was going to write and thank you for the Valentine, and then I fell and didn't get to do it. But it meant so much to me. It was the only Valentine I received. In fact, it is the first one I have received in years."

When an elderly couple who had received a card came by to speak to us at church on Sunday, the man threw his arms around my wife and kissed her. "Thanks for the pretty Valentine," he said.

All the Valentines together cost maybe seven or eight dollars, and another dollar or two for the stamps. But what happiness they brought—more than an equal number of pastoral visits!

A Little Something Sweet

My wife loves to cook, and now that our boys are gone from home she feels deprived. At special times of the year she makes up for it by baking cookies or cakes or making candies for our older friends.

One friend is named Jo Banks. Jo was a professor in a boy's school for years and years. When he retired, he moved to a farm, then back to a retirement home across the street from the school where he taught. His room there is filled with memorabilia, including a number of clocks from a large collection he developed through the years. He keeps a sheet of paper taped to the window of his sixth-floor residence so boys from his old school can always identify it from the ground and wave as they pass. Jo is a rugged old individualist who quotes Browning, feeds a pet crow outside named Samuel, and generally seems to dislike women. The first Christmas I was his pastor, he gave me a little tree branch tacked to a base, with a lone bullet tied to it. It bore a card with the caption, "Cartridge in a Bare Tree."

My wife is one of the few women Jo seems to like. She responds by sending him fudge at Christmas or on his birthday. She always sends enough so that he can pass it out to anyone who stops by his room. A few days after I take it to him, a card arrives, addressed to my wife. It simply says, "Thanks. Banks."

Other friends receive pies or congo squares or lemon cookies. Usually at Christmas and at Eastertime I find myself driving around with several plates of goodies for our elderly friends, each gaily wrapped in paper and ribbons. It is such a little thing to do, but it seems to bring great happiness into our friends' lives. The pastor and his wife are, after all, sacramental figures. Their attention means a lot.

V

Developing Fellowship

The spirit of fellowship in a congregation is intangible, but you can tell whether it is there or not. You can almost tell it when you walk in the church door, from the way people greet one another or speak to strangers. You can certainly tell it in small group gatherings such as church school classes and in the worship service itself. It all has to do with the degrees of love and comfort people feel with one another. Most people are capable of fellowship, but sometimes it has to be drawn out of them. They need the assurance that it is all right to be open and friendly, and that other people will meet them halfway if they are outgoing. If they believe that the atmosphere is right, and that their own efforts will be received graciously, they will be more than willing to do their part. In fact, they will be delighted to do it, because they know how rare real fellowship is in the world we inhabit today.

The pastor of a congregation has two primary goals when it comes to fellowship. One is to promote a general sense of fellowship so that everyone feels the ambience of care and worth which invites participation; and the second is to be sure that literally everyone is included in the sense of fellowship and there are no enclaves or inner circles where newcomers and strangers are not welcome.

Both goals are easier in small congregations than large ones. Large churches can often seem forbidding to newcomers. They can also foster the need of certain members to band together in cliques or limited-interest groups for the sake of identity and security. But even in larger congregations it is possible to achieve an air of warmth and familiarity, so that people do not feel threatened and standoffish. And the pastor is the key person to see that this air is created.

Thinking Fellowship on Sunday Morning

Fellowship in a church begins by the pastor's "thinking" it on Sunday morning. If it is not in the pastor's mind, if it does not come out in the pastor's speech and gestures and way of looking at the congregation, it is not likely to develop at all. A cold, unresponsive pastor usually leads to a cold, unresponsive congregation, or at least to one that *seems* cold and unresponsive.

It isn't always easy to be "up" for the Sunday service. The pastor is human, like everyone else, and will have bad days. I remember a Protestant minister who had just heard of Low Sunday, the Sunday after Easter. "A lot of mine are like that," he said. He was probably thinking of days when he didn't feel well, or when he wasn't really prepared to preach, or when the church board had recently voted not to give him a raise because the church finances were in a bad way.

But it is important, despite how we feel, that we convey a sense of love and warmth on Sunday morning. The glow on the minister's face as he or she sits in the chancel is fully as instrumental in helping people worship as the lilt of the music or the attractiveness of the decor. I am often sorry this is so, because there are times when I simply don't feel like glowing. But there are other times when I am glad it is so, because it means that I can help overcome the effects of a hymn people didn't know and couldn't sing or of a gloomy day that turns all the stained glass to dark, brooding colors.

When I come out and take my seat a few minutes before the Introit and processional, I always look around the sanctuary and smile at people. (I find this more useful than seeming to pray, which in many ministers strikes me as an affectation.) I smile and exchange winks with many of the choir members as they file past into the chancel, singing as they come. And I always try to beam a little warmth in the direction of parents who are waiting for their children's baptisms, of the acolytes who sit on the center aisle of the first pew, and of my wife, who is likely to be seated anywhere in the sanctuary, as she tries to move around and sit with various friends from Sunday to Sunday. Smiling is sacramental to me. It is a way I have of letting the love of God loose in the congregation. If I don't do it, I have to assume that it may not get loose on a particular Sunday.

We always greet our friends and visitors during the worship service, after the call to worship, processional hymn, opening prayer, first anthem, and confession of sin. My associate pastor would like to do it before the service begins, and have the announcements then too, but I resist moving these matters outside the perimeters of worship. There was a time when I would have agreed with him. I can still agree with him in principle. But over the years I have come to believe even more strongly in the principle of love and fellowship in worship. Of course God should be central to everything we do and think in worship. But Louis Evely is right, I think, that it is God who is doing something for us when we worship, not the other way around. We like to think we are serving God, and perhaps we are, in a way; yet the service of God has always been such that it blesses the server more than the One served. So I have come to regard the moments of speaking directly to the congregation about how welcome they are and what the church is up to during the week as sacred moments deserving a place not at the edge of worship but in its middle.

Our greeting is never effusive—we are Presbyterians!—but I hope it is always warm and truly welcoming. We pass our Friendship Books down the pews, urge people to linger after the service, say how glad we are to have visitors, either in the sanctuary or by radio, and comment briefly on the upcoming opportunities for the week, especially those involving the entire congregation. If it is possible to include a bit of humor during any of these remarks, we do so, on the theory that humor is a sign of openness and good will, a gesture of kindness and grace.

We don't want people to think we are God's frozen people. We don't even want to convey the impression that we think we're God's chosen people. We *do* want them to feel that they are among the chosen—that God has chosen them and we are choosing them too!

If there isn't an atmosphere of fellowship in the worship service, there probably is not very much of it anywhere else in the church.

Punch and Cookies in the Narthex

Following each Sunday service, we have punch and cookies in the narthex and encourage both members and visitors to linger for a few minutes to greet one another. We are fortunate to have an extremely large narthex, purposely designed for this. Our Fellowship Mission Group is responsible for preparing the table of refreshments and cleaning up afterward. A different family or combination of families assumes the duty each month.

Even though ours is a large city church, it often reminds me of small rural churches I have known where people liked to stay for half an hour after church and visit. It is a rare occasion if my wife and I get away from the narthex before twelve forty-five. The children consume far more of the punch and cookies than the adults, I suspect; but everyone seems to relish the informal atmosphere and the sheer joy of seeing everyone else.

Meeting the Pastor's Wife (or Husband)

The lovely wife of one of our former pastors always stood with him at the door to greet people after church, and we invariably enjoyed seeing her as well as him.

When we arrived at this parish, my wife and I agreed that she should join me at the door.

It took some getting used to for some folks. For a few Sundays, they would stare awkwardly at my wife as they plunged past her to take my hand and speak to me. Eventually, however, they came to regard it as a treat to see her there, and she received as many hugs and kisses and handshakes as I did. In fact, I am sure the older men much prefer to see her, and many of them are extremely pleased when she teases them.

I find it a great help to have her present with me. She learns many things during the course of the greetings that I would not learn, and later, at the dinner table, we usually compare notes on who is having what problem and which persons I ought to see during the coming week.

There is one other benefit of this husband-and-wife arrangement: it says volumes about the solidarity of the minister's family and helps set an example of real togetherness for other couples in the community. And, for what it is worth, it reduces the vulnerability of the minister to persons of the opposite sex!

Guess Who's Coming to Dinner

In a large church, for many persons the only contact with the body of Christ is on Sunday morning when they come to worship. What can be done to widen the circle of their acquaintances and give them a feeling of really belonging to the fellowship of the saints in a local church?

Perhaps the most successful answer to this question in our church has been the formation of an informal program called "Hearthsiders." It is entirely voluntary and by no means embraces the entire congregation. The first time it was announced only fifty people signed up for it. Six months later, when we were reorganizing, word of the program had got around and a hundred signed up. Six months later we were up to a hundred and thirty.

Hearthsiders is a voluntary dinner association. It takes the names of all the participants, scrambles them, and realigns them in groups of eight for monthly shared dinners. For purposes of grouping, single persons are usually put together as couples and the names arranged according to couples. (We have had singles, however, who desired to function alone, as though they were couples.) If there are enough participants in the program, the names can be arranged so that a couple (or single) eats with three different couples each month for the entire year.

My wife helped devise the method of arrangement when we were members of a small church in another city. She and three other women "invented" the program we use—it was called "Salt Shakers" in that church—and the actual charts for "shaking up" the membership were devised by Mr. George Boyles, a retired layman with a penchant for mathematics.

Each couple (or single) in the program is assigned a number. The numbers are then arranged in four vertical columns, and in such a way that they appear each time, when read horizontally, with three numbers they have not previously been grouped with. Persons in the first column each month are the "host" couple; they provide the place to meet (normally their own home), the meat dish, starchy vegetable, and drinks. Persons in the second column bring the green vegetable. Those in the third column furnish salad and bread. And the ones in the fourth column bring dessert. If the numbers are properly arranged, each couple serves as host only once every fourth month. Thus the burden of the meal is always distributed, so that no couple or individual has too much responsibility.

There is no agenda for these monthly dinner parties except to eat and visit. This, our people have found, is the beauty of Hearthsiders. Most of them, among community, school, work, and church, are nearly programmed to death. Hearthsiders gives them a relaxed time in which to become better acquainted with one another, tell stories, and chat about the things they feel like discussing. The payoff, in any congregation, is in terms of people getting to know one another. In a year's time, each couple gets to spend an evening with thirty-three other couples.

It has been our experience that the evenings often lead to further meetings and friendships. A Rotarian will discover a prospective new Rotarian. A woman with a passion for gardening will find another devotee. Cooks call each other to exchange recipes. Golfers make golf dates. Hunters plan hunting trips.

"I would have been lost without Hearthsiders," said one man in our church. "I've come to know more people here in six months than I knew in my last church after six years."

"The greatest thing since sliced bread!" said another person. "I wasn't so sure when we signed up. I thought I needed another evening out like I needed a hole in the head. But I can hardly wait each month for the next meeting. I've come to know some wonderful people!"

A program like Hearthsiders has to be talked up, advertised, and explained. And it requires a good bit of work each year for someone to arrange the names and numbers, type, print, and distribute the master sheets to all the participants. But once it is established, and all the sheets are out, it is virtually self-sustaining.

We can save you the most difficult task by offering on the following pages the general directions and the master charts devised by George Boyles. The charts are designed to accommodate programs of various sizes. One is for twenty-four persons, one for forty, and one for sixty-four. What we do, for larger programs, is to combine two or more of these. If you are a mathematician and enjoy working out combinations you can devise your own chart. Or, if you have a computer, you can easily plan it all by machine.

Two other comments:

1. The host couple is responsible each month for phoning the other couples in the group and arranging the time of the dinner. Our people have found that it is good to arrange their dinners a month in advance; otherwise they run into congested schedules.

2. When we ask people to sign up for Hearthsiders, we also ask for those who wish to be involved in an "alternate" capacity. This is for persons who do not think they can spare an evening a month for the program but would like to be called occasionally as fill-ins when another couple cannot make it. Then we publish an "alternates" list with the regular list.

Directions for Hearthsiders

1 The dinner groups for each month are determined by reading across from left to right. The names of participants, corresponding with the numbers on the chart, are on an accompanying sheet.

2 The part of the dinner for which each couple or single is responsible each month is determined by the vertical columns. Reading the columns from left to right:

Column 1—The host is responsible for the date, time, and place; entree; complementary vegetable (rice or potatoes); and beverage. *It is a good idea to start early in the month to set a date.* Call each person in your group.

Column 2—Vegetable

Column 3—Salad and bread

Column 4—Dessert

3 Dinner hosts are encouraged to invite new or prospective church members to come as guests to any dinner group.

4 If a regular member of your group cannot attend, call an alternate.

The Best Dinners We've Ever Had

In addition to Hearthsiders, of course, our church has monthly fellowship dinners to which everyone is invited. I personally envy those churches that have regular dietitians and can sponsor such a dinner once a week. But we have found that monthly dinners are a great improvement over the annual fund-raising dinners that were customary when we arrived in our parish. They give folks an opportunity to gather in a relaxed,

Developing Fellowship

Schedule for 12 Couples

1st month	2nd month	3rd month
1 4 7 10	5 9 12 1	8 11 1 6
2 5 8 11	6 7 11 2	9 12 2 4
3 6 9 12	4 8 10 3	7 10 3 5

4th month	5th month	6th month
1 2 3 10	5 9 12 1	6 11 1 8
4 5 6 11	8 3 10 4	9 12 4 2
7 8 9 12	2 6 11 7	3 10 7 5

Schedule for 20 Couples

1st month	2nd month	3rd month
1 6 11 16	19 1 7 13	15 17 1 8
2 7 12 17	20 2 8 14	11 18 2 9
3 8 13 18	16 3 9 15	12 19 3 10
4 9 14 19	17 4 10 11	13 20 4 6
5 10 15 20	18 5 6 12	14 16 5 7

4th month	5th month	6th month
9 12 20 1	1 10 14 18	1 2 3 4
10 13 16 2	2 6 15 19	5 6 7 8
6 14 17 3	3 7 11 20	9 10 11 12
7 15 18 4	4 8 12 16	13 14 15 16
8 11 19 5	5 9 13 17	17 18 19 20

Schedule for 32 Couples

1st month	2nd month	3rd month
1 9 17 25	10 19 28 1	21 31 1 11
2 10 18 26	11 20 29 2	22 32 2 12
3 11 19 27	12 21 30 3	23 25 3 13
4 12 20 28	13 22 31 4	24 26 4 14
5 13 21 29	14 23 32 5	17 27 5 15
6 14 22 30	15 24 25 6	18 28 6 16
7 15 23 31	16 17 26 7	19 29 7 9
8 16 24 32	9 18 27 8	20 30 8 10

4th month	5th month	6th month
26 1 12 23	1 13 18 30	14 20 27 1
27 2 13 24	2 14 19 31	15 21 28 2
28 3 14 17	3 15 20 32	16 22 29 3
29 4 15 18	4 16 21 25	9 23 30 4
30 5 16 19	5 9 22 26	10 24 31 5
31 6 9 20	6 10 23 27	11 17 32 6
32 7 10 21	7 11 24 28	12 18 25 7
25 8 11 22	8 12 17 29	13 19 26 8

noncritical setting and to enjoy an evening of food, fellowship, fun, and inspiration together.

We have tried both catered dinners and potluck dinners, and have found that almost everybody prefers the latter. They give people a chance to try out their best or newest dishes, and the results have been fabulous. Some of the best dinners any of us have ever eaten have been in the fellowship hall of the church! And some people are extremely thoughtful of the children; while others are bringing gourmet casseroles and salads, they bring huge containers of fried chicken or frankfurters.

One of these days we shall have to publish a cookbook of recipes from our dinners. Many churches do this, and it is a popular way to raise money or generate interest in the dinners. For the time being, we have a lot of phoning and passing back and forth of recipes—a helpful by-product of the dinners that continues to bring people together long after the dinners are over.

We try to have an interesting, enjoyable program to follow each dinner, usually featuring people in our own congregation. There are plays, musicals, grab bags of readings and songs, slide shows, and even an occasional lecture. One of the most popular features has been the showing of silent movies, with our minister of music, who once played in movie houses in England, accompanying them on the piano. We aim for variety in programming, never following a "heavy" program with another heavy. We try to have something the children will enjoy as much as the adults. And we attempt to finish everything by eight o'clock, so that our students can get home to the books and those who have other programs to attend in the city can get there on time.

As a pastor, I have found that fellowship dinners are one of the best places for beginning to integrate new members into the congregation. We always urge them, when they join our church, to attend the dinners. We introduce them to the crowd at the dinners, both individually and at the time of general greetings and remarks. And they invariably seem to make the kinds of contacts there that lead to further involvement in the life of our people.

How About Lunch?

In these busy times, when even minutes are at a premium in most people's schedules, lunch is an invaluable opportunity for the pastor to have fellowship with businesspersons. Our church staff has a brown-bag lunch together on Mondays, preceding our joint staff meeting, and occasionally I try to have lunch with my wife. But many other luncheon periods are consumed by appointments with busy men or women—mostly men—I probably couldn't see otherwise.

Sometimes there is an agenda for these luncheons—I need to talk with the chairperson of the Christian Education Mission Group or a member of the Every-Member Canvass Committee. But usually they are merely for visiting and being together. We talk about our families, things happening in the other person's work, books we've been reading, unusual experiences we've had since the last time we were together. I particularly like to keep in touch this way with some of the newer Christians in the congregation, to see that they are moving along in their spiritual pilgrimages and aren't having trouble with barriers along the way. When lunch is over and I return to the church, I invariably feel that the time has been well spent.

Occasionally I try to get a small group together for lunch—perhaps four or five elders, or three or four younger church members, or some doctors or lawyers—and use the time to relax together, to suggest something they could be doing for the church, or to invite their comments on how things are going in the congregation. The fallout from these occasions is always good. I can feel it for weeks when I see them casually in the church line or at a meeting. It creates a bond among us.

It was not a mere accident of history that one of our two primary sacraments in the church became centered on a table!

Receptions for Special Groups

Here is one we haven't gotten around to yet in our church, but its on the agenda for sometime in the future. We often have receptions centered on special persons, especially employees joining or leaving the staff. Why not have receptions embracing whole groups of persons who have something in common, for example, secretaries, engineers, teachers, artists, pianists, authors and scribblers, widows under sixty, single parents, people with September birthdays?

Preparations wouldn't have to be elaborate: an announced time and place; a nice table setting; coffee, tea, juice, and cookies; name tags for everyone; and perhaps some good background music. The artists could set up their own exhibit and look at one another's works. Authors might have a display of some of their favorite books. Others might listen to an appropriate speaker for ten minutes and then mingle and talk as they pleased.

An active fellowship group in a church could plan at least one such reception every month that would serve the purpose of introducing people with similar interests to one another. An alert pastor would also discover talents and interests in people that had been previously unknown.

Having Fun at a Meeting

One of the often overlooked places for real fellowship in every church is the board or committee meeting. We have become conditioned to think of meetings as obligations to be discharged, and therefore mere necessary evils. This may be true of some meetings, but there is no reason it should be true of those in the church. When Christians gather for any purpose there should be a touch of joy and delight in the occasion.

Pastors ought to be alert to the opportunity of turning meetings into genuine fellowship times for those who attend. The spirit in which the meetings are conducted should be at once gentle, spirited, happy, and positive. A smiling leader, a well-planned agenda, a firm but tender hand in moving things along, and a happy voice with affirmative things to say will do much to lift the hearts of all those present and to ensure their enjoying one another's company.

I was immensely pleased by something one of our officers said at a recent board meeting. We were discussing the possibility of having only one meeting a month instead of two, a possibility introduced by the excellent way the board's subcommittees have been handling their business so that it does not demand the attention of the full board. "I wouldn't want to go to a single meeting a month," said this particular officer, "because I would miss the fellowship of this group. I genuinely enjoy coming to these meetings and don't want to be deprived of your company."

There are little "externals" that help produce good feelings at meetings—pleasant decor in a room, tea and coffee, cakes or cookies occasionally. But the important ingredient is the tone set by the leaders. If it is friendly and upbeat, work times will become fun times.

Take Me Out to the Ball Game

Intramural and extramural sports events are something still on the drawing board for us, but they too can be very instrumental in helping congregants get to know one another. I look lustfully in the direction of churches that have their own gymnasiums and sports areas. How wonderful it would be, I think, to have a church-sponsored calendar of volleyball, tennis, badminton, softball, and basketball games!

I reflect on the indoor tennis club where I have a winter contract with five other players. There is always an air of excitement in the place. The smell is special. The sound of tennis balls being whack! whack! whacked with rhythmic intensity, the punctuation of the air by shouts of enthusiastic players, the noise of pounding feet on the courts, all contribute to a unique feeling in the club, as if one is absorbed into a kind of sacramental fellowship merely by entering, by joining the force field of perspiring bodies and wildly pumping hearts. The men I play with are among my closest friends in the city. We are bonded by what we do together.

Why shouldn't churches take advantage of this kind of bonding in their fellowship programs? It isn't necessary to have gyms and ball fields. There are plenty of these around, and squash and racquetball courts and swimming pools and bowling alleys and skating rinks too. All that's required is a committed sports organizer or two who will take the time to arrange competitions and places for them to be staged. Prizes and awards are not necessary. The real prize is the added dimension this brings to the church's fellowship.

Picnics and Ice Cream Socials

Ours is an urban congregation with all the sophistication befitting a big-steeple church, but we still enjoy some of the down-home pleasures when it comes to fellowship. One is an old-fashioned picnic.

We began our annual June picnic one summer when several of the people in our church were on a presbytery-wide committee to raise funds for a new lodge at our run-down presbytery camp. The best way to fire people's imagination for the fund drive, we thought, was to get them down to the camp and let them see what it could be like. So we arranged to have a picnic there after church on Sunday and invited everybody to come to church in picnicky clothes. After the service we left the church building and traveled in a caravan into the country to spend the afternoon together.

People were asked to bring their own lunches, and the church provided drinks. The church also provided ice-cold watermelons, and a restaurant-owner member gave us more Howard Johnson's ice cream than we could possibly consume. After the picnic lunch an entertainment committee supervised games—volleyball, foot races, three-legged races, sack races, horseshoes, frisbee toss. There were swimming, canoeing, and much talking by those who sat on the banks of the lake and watched. There was a hayride of sorts—a tour of the extensive campgrounds (which, incidentally, are in a lovely mountain setting)—on a large wagon pulled by a wheezing old tractor.

It was a perfect afternoon, and most people said they hadn't had so much fun in years. They wanted to know if we could have this every year. And we have, every year since. One of our amateur photographers took dozens of pictures of scenes at the picnic which were displayed in the church foyer for everyone to see, drawing many new people the second year. It was a splendid intergenerational event!

Why must we wait till next year? asked some folks who thought such good times ought to come more frequently. Why can't we have another event this summer? So we did. In\early August, we had an old-fashioned ice-cream social at the church, with cakes and cookies and soft drinks and ice cream—lots and lots of ice cream. And we had entertainment—music and films and jokes and merriment. And now we have an ice-cream social every year as well as a picnic. When church families begin having fun together, there is no stopping them!

Everybody Should Have a Homecoming

Thomas Wolfe not withstanding, there is nothing like a homecoming to generate excitement in a local church. Our church had never had a homecoming in its more than one hundred years' existence, not even for its centennial. Then, when Mrs. Fannie Moore was about to turn one hundred, we decided to have one. Our Fellowship Mission Group was asked to take charge of the homecoming dinner, and *ad hoc* program and finance committees were appointed. Publicity was generated, first in the church and then in the community. It was Miz Fannie's Day, we said, but it was also *our* day.

Probably there had never been another day like it in the history of our church. The sanctuary was nearly filled for the eight-forty-five service. Church school was canceled so people could visit in the narthex and halls between services and greet the popular former ministers. By ten minutes till eleven, the sanctuary was already filled again, and chairs began going up in the aisles and narthex. At five after twelve, people poured into the Fellowship Hall, where a team of many persons had been preparing plates of fried chicken and hot biscuits and vegetables. No one knew the hall could hold so many people, but everyone who wanted to come was accommodated. Tables had to be set even on the stage, and Miz Fannie and her family were up there. A birthday cake was the centerpiece of every table, and teenagers squeezed among the tables carrying trays with dishes of several kinds of ice cream. We had speeches by friends and members of Miz Fannie's family, and then Fannie herself wanted the microphone to tell a humorous story. Everyone applauded, and afterward many crowded around to congratulate her, overjoyed to be basking in the radiance of her celebration.

"I have been a member here all my life," said one woman, "and I have never felt such love and enthusiasm in this congregation before."

"It was a feast of the Spirit," said someone else. "I'll never forget it, even if I live to be as old as Miz Fannie!"

It *was* special. For a day, or a week, or maybe even a month, an uptown city church, that probably thought it was above such things, had the experience of warmth and fellowship that is much more common to small rural churches where people live as extended families in Christ. It did us good. Friendships were renewed, people spoke to people they hadn't spoken to in ages, and a sense of the church as the people of God was rekindled in all of us.

Maybe every church ought to have a homecoming!

VI

Promoting Spiritual Growth

"A congregation's spiritual life seldom rises above the level of its pastor's devotional life."

Several years ago I copied this sentence out of the prayer journal of one of my students. It has since been in one of my notebooks to accuse me every time I happen upon it. I hope it is not true, but I fear that it is. Whether it is or not, it keeps me working at my own spiritual life, which can easily become a casualty of life in the Christian ministry.

It is easy, in the ministry, to get faked out of one's primary work. So many things demand our attention that we can soon forget our original goals. Making the wheels turn can become a substitute for arriving at our real destination. I once kept a diary of all the things I had to do in a week and though I was familiar with my ordinary working days I was nevertheless amazed at the sheer number of things absorbing my time and energy. There were numerous conferences with individual staff members, visits with parishioners, phone calls, letters, memos, luncheons, dinners, a breakfast or two, meetings with salespersons, representatives of local agencies, and other ministers, responses to reporters, crisis calls, funerals, weddings, announcements, sermons—the list went on and on. My life's blood seemed to be leaking out at every pore! If I didn't work hard at my devotional life, I knew, I would soon become all periphery without a center, an empty shell, a mockery as a servant of Christ.

So I have tried to shore up my inner life with prayer time, reading, study, travel, and habits of reflection and renewal. The hours for this are never enough, but I constantly work at it. Vacation days have become revival and recommitment times for me. I tell my elders that the church gets more of its money's worth out of me when I am on vacation than at any other time. I always come back from a trip with new sermons, prayers, illustrations, and ideas for redesigning our parish life. At least my time away helps offset the debilitating effect of a too-harried schedule and reinforces the sense of God's presence and guidance I feel in my less ample devotional moments at home.

Armed with a semblance of my own spiritual life, I turn to the congregation. What can I do to raise my people's consciousness of the inner life and its importance in their daily existence? How can I help them become more reflective as Christians, so that their discipleship is more autonomous and less dependent on the pleas and proddings of their pastors?

When I was a professor in the divinity school, I had many long conversations with other professors as we attempted to identify our aim in theological education. Finally, we summarized our intention in this manner: What we wanted to do was to turn our students into *theologians*. That is, we decided it was not enough merely to fill the students' heads with the variety of knowledge we professors had to impart—church history, biblical studies, historical and systematic theology, Christian ethics, pastoral care, homiletics and liturgics, and all the rest. If that was all we did, the students would be obsolete in twenty years, and, in the meantime, would be completely baffled by every pastoral or ecclesiastical problem that did not fit neatly within the template of the information they were carrying around. What we had to do was something more. We had to equip them to think theologically for themselves, to be able to approach any problem or situation and handle it as deftly or creatively as their professors might. We wanted them to go out not as parrots but as thinkers.

Surely this is what we wish to achieve with the people in our parishes—not to make automata of them, dependent on our exhorting and interpretations of everything, but to help them become spiritual and theological followers in their own right. We want to enable them to make their own pilgrimages—within the context of the Christian community, of course—and to attain ever higher levels of individual devotion and critical ability in the faith. Then the entire community will profit from constant stimulation and growth, and we pastors will be freer to turn our attention to new and more adventurous areas of service.

Beginning with Worship

The natural place to begin working at our people's spiritual and theological quotients is of course in our worship itself. There is a reciprocal relationship between worship and the other areas of parish life, so that what is done in either automatically affects the other. But, as more of our parishioners are involved in weekly worship than in any other program of the congregation, worship is the easiest point at which to start. What we do there begins immediately to affect the tone and style of everything else.

As a former professor of preaching and worship who has worshiped in many settings with many kinds of congregations, I am convinced that the problem with most liturgies is not as much with their arrangements, which may vary greatly, as with the quality of their individual parts. Almost any liturgy that provides for proclamation, confession, adoration, thanksgiving, and supplication, *and that flows well from beginning to end,* is a suitable vehicle for the transaction we hope will occur during Christian worship. But, by the same token, any liturgy whose contents are not fresh and meaningful will fail in the transaction, regardless of how well it is planned and arranged. The secret of successful worship, aside from the sheer intervention of the Holy Spirit, lies in the freshness and suitability of its parts.

We have made it a practice in our church, therefore, to work diligently at the preparation of our worship services, spending perhaps inordinate amounts of time on prayers, responses, affirmations, and other "variables" of the weekly liturgies. In all of them, we aim at a "high colloquialism" in the language—enough of the semblance of daily speech to identify them easily with the lives and experiences of our people, yet chaste and elevated enough to draw people's attention and feelings toward the Holy at the center of worship. We try to reflect the common, daily life of the people, so that they are readily drawn into the process of worship; yet we attempt to turn all their cares and interests in bona fide theological directions, so that they come out at new levels with post-resurrection interpretations.

Although we use the Apostles' Creed often enough for people to feel that it is staple confession of our faith, we frequently employ new creeds so that they will have a sense of the dynamism and openness of the faith. Here, for example, are affirmations we have used at Christmas and Easter:

A CHRISTMAS AFFIRMATION

I believe that Christmas is more than a time for parties and ornaments; it is a time for remembering Christ and the incarnation of God's love in human flesh.

I believe there are gifts more important than the ones under the Christmas tree, such as the things we teach our children, the way we share ourselves with friends, and the industry with which we set about reshaping the world in our time.

I believe that the finest carols are often sung by the poorest voices, from hearts made warm by the wonder of the season.

I believe in the angel's message that we should not be

afraid—that the Child of Bethlehem is able to overcome all anxieties and insecurities.

I believe in prayer and quietness as a way of appropriating Christmas—that if I wait in silence I will experience the presence of the One born in the stable, for he lives today as surely as he lived then.

I believe in going away from Christmas as the Wise Men went—"another way." I want to be different when these days are past—more centered, more thoughtful, more caring.

And I believe God will help me. Amen.

AN EASTER AFFIRMATION

I believe in the beauty of spring that is known in windy skies, blossoming fruit trees, waving jonquils, and sweet-smelling grass;

I believe in the warmth of friendship that is communicated in gentle eyes, a loving smile, a fond touch of the hand, and an arm laid on the shoulder.

I believe in the power of Christ whose presence is felt in every season of the year but especially now, when life wells up everywhere and folks feel a quickening in their souls because it is spring and summer is on the way.

I believe Christ is somehow responsible for both spring and friendship, and that the excitement I feel today is related to the fact that he was dead but is alive forevermore, not only in our memories but in the truest kind of actuality.

I worship him by coming here, and say, "Hallelujah! Christ is alive, and in this very place." Amen.

We also frequently use congregational dialogues or litanies in our services to celebrate special occasions or to say hello or good-bye to special persons in our lives. Here is the farewell dialogue that was employed as part of our worship when our associate pastor, Dr. Robert Bullock, and his family left us to become the founding family of a new church in Allen, Texas:

The Tender Shepherd

Leader: *For many years, Jesus Christ has called men and women to be ministers of the gospel, preaching and teaching and administering the sacraments.*

People: The work is endless and worldwide.

Leader: *The leadership of the Holy Spirit has taken them to many places, in Africa, and Asia, and Allen, Texas.*

People: Leaving is never easy, for ministers or their congregations.

Leader: *Lives have grown together, and roots have become established.*

People: Yet we all belong to God, and want to follow God's will.

Leader: *Therefore, Robert and Gretchen and Richard, we accept your need to take up a new work.*

People: Even though it gives us inward pain, we wish you well in your new calling.

Leader: *We shall remember you in our prayers, and hope you will remember us in yours.*

People: We support you with our affection as you go.

Leader: *We commend you to God and God's people in Allen.*

People: We shall follow your work there with interest.

Leader: *We shall keep here a place of retreat whenever you want to return.*

People: We shall receive you as one of our own, which you are.

Leader: *May God go with you and crown your efforts with great success.*

People: May our paths cross again on the great journey of life.

Together: And may Jesus Christ be praised! Amen.

Always, the emphasis is upon trying to set whatever we are focusing upon in the context of the Christian faith and in the presence of God. The intention is to help people see that the particularities of their own existence should be viewed in a similar way.

We try to bring the same kind of freshness to our treatment of the sacraments and preaching. The forms for baptism and the Lord's Supper, both incorporated into morning worship, are often altered to prevent their becoming stale or unnoticed. The Lord's Supper is celebrated in three ways: On the first Sunday of each month and on Christmas Eve, when the crowds are largest, it is served in the pews by our elders; on Maundy Thursday people come forward during a time of meditation and serve themselves at a low table (designed for kneeling) before the chancel steps; and on Thanksgiving Day it is offered by intinction, with the pastors holding the chalices while the people dip their bread into the wine.

I plan my preaching emphases three months in advance and strive to achieve a good balance among pastoral, prophetic, and doctrinal sermons, with every sermon, regardless of its overall style or emphasis, strongly oriented toward pastoral ministry. Pastoral and doctrinal sermons often deal with subjects related to personal and spiritual growth. Two or three years ago, for example, I preached a series of sermons on prayer which was subsequently published as *The Cup and the Waterfall* (Ramsey, N.J.: Paulist Press, 1983). I have also preached series on love, death and the afterlife, and Christian marriage. (The reader who wishes to know more about my preaching practices is directed to my book *The Fundamentals of Preaching* [Philadelphia: Fortress Press, 1985].)

We have tried to be sensitive to our parishioners and what *they* find meaningful in worship services. To this end, we recently developed a worship questionnaire, which was placed in the pew racks each Sunday for a month. Parishioners were urged to complete one questionnaire each. Our Worship Mission Group is presently studying the tabulated results and remarks from the questionnaires and will recommend alterations in our liturgical practices, either experimentally or semipermanently, as it sees fit. Here is the form we devised:

HOW DO *YOU* FEEL ABOUT OUR WORSHIP?

The Worship Mission Group of our church desires your input. Please complete one of these forms during March and place it in the box in the narthex or return to the church office. You may sign or not sign your name, as you please.

1. Are you generally satisfied with the order of worship used in our worship services? _____ Yes   _____ No
   If not, would you please say why? _____

2. What do you like most about the order of worship?
   _____

What do you like least? _____

3. Do you find the saying of the Apostles' Creed:
   _____ Meaningful   _____Not very meaningful   _____
   Less than "Not very meaningful"?

4. How do you feel about the use of contemporary creeds, which are often substituted for the Apostles' Creed?
   _____ Good _____ Indifferent   _____ Bad

5. Do the congregational hymns usually: _____ Help you worship God   _____ Interfere with your sense of worship? If they interfere, would you please say in what way?
   _____

   _____

6. Do you find the choir music (introits, anthems, responses) generally: _____ Helpful and uplifting _____
   Distracting _____ Other? Why? _____

   _____

7. Do you value the Prayer of Confession and Words of Assurance often used in our services? _____ Yes _____ No
   Again, would you please say why?

   _____

8. Do you find the sermons you normally hear in our services: _____ Helpful and inspiring _____ Not very helpful _____ Useless and tedious? If one of the latter two responses, would you please try to explain?_____

_____

9. Have you suggestions for subjects you would like to hear discussed in sermons? ——————————————

_____

10. Have you suggestions for hymns you would like to have used more often in our services? _____

_____

11. Do you value monthly communion over quarterly communion? _____ Yes _____ No Would you please say why? _____

_____

12. Do you feel that the use of acolytes to light and extinguish the candles in the chancel is: _____ Desirable _____ Undesirable? If undesirable, would you please say why? _____

_____

13. Do you find the prayers used in our services generally: _____ Helpful and devotional _____ Not very helpful? If the latter, would you please say why?
_____

_____

14. Do you enjoy using the "Edelweiss" benediction sung by the congregation? _____ Yes _____ No

15. Do you prefer having the "Christian Concerns" (passing our Friendship Books, announcements, etc.) in the: _____ Middle of the service where they now are _____ At the beginning of the service before the Call to Worship? Would you say why? _____

_____

16. Do you enjoy the Preludes and Postludes? _____ Yes _____ No If not, would you please say why? _____

_____

17. Do you think we have enough special services (Ash Wednesday, Maundy Thursday, Thanksgiving, Christmas Eve, Annual Preaching Series, etc.) each year or should there be more? _____ Enough _____ More

18. Do you find the time of silence before the Corporate Prayer helpful to your worship? _____ Yes _____ No If not, would you please say why? _____

_____

19. Are our bulletins attractive enough for your taste? _____ Yes _____ No If not, would you please make suggestions for improving them? _____

_____

20. Do you think the length of our scripture readings is generally: _____ Too long _____ Too short _____ About right?

21. Please use the remaining space to make any comments or write any suggestions you may have regarding our worship services:

_____

_____

_____

_____

(Use the back of this page)

Developing a Sacramental Attitude

Through our liturgies and other means, we hope to develop in our people a sacramental attitude toward all of life. We would like them to regard their families as the matrices of spiritual growth and their work as an opportunity to see and respond to God in the world. We want them to see other people's faces as the faces of God, and nature as the garden where God visits his children. We hope they will come to view paintings, films, and books as theological statements, and travel as a kind of religious pilgrimage.

One way of doing this is to bring as much of the world as possible into the church and study and enjoy it there. We have had courses in religion and politics, religion and literature, and religion and television. We look forward to courses in religion and art, religion and music, and religion and medicine. We also anticipate the day when we shall have regular art shows, drama festivals, craft fairs, food fairs, travel seminars, legislative conferences, and other manifestations of our care for the world and the way faith, hope, and love are mediated in the secular context.

Because art and creativity are so closely allied to the nature of God and the Christian experience, we like to see our people as creatively involved in the church as possible. In addition to involving them in art, music, and drama, we ask them to produce materials for the Advent and Lenten devotional booklets. There is nothing more thrilling to me as a pastor than to read the devotional

[103]

thoughts of homemakers, salespersons, students, medical doctors, bankers, and secretaries that are set forth inexpensively in a church-produced pamphlet.

Here from one of our Advent booklets, for example, is the devotional penned by Mrs. Helen Newbold, who is secretary for another church in our city:

Luke 2:1-20

The shepherds were tending their flocks, and the angels appeared to them. They were not in the temple or even at prayer. They were at work—and behold! a surprise visit from the Lord!

God is full of such surprise visits. No angels or burning bush for us. But God does visit us in the midst of our daily routine. He surprises us again and again. We need only be aware.

We can see him in the baby's tears, the client's demands, the household routine, the patient's fears, the shopping lines—in the most unlikely places. And he turns our lives around!

God will surely surprise you with a visit today. Watch for him!

PRAYER: *I go about my work today, O Lord, eagerly awaiting your surprise visits. Amen.*

Such booklets are marvelous pastoral devices. They permit us to tap on the shoulder dozens of people who might otherwise have no way of contributing to the general life of the congregation and then to share with everyone the produce of their hearts and minds. They are especially useful in drawing in the sensitive, artistic souls who are often introverted or remain on the periphery of church activities and giving them a sense of belonging. And of course the booklets are meaningful to all the other church members who use them as the basis for daily devotions for an entire season of the church year!

The Ministry of Retreats

John Westerhoff, the renowned lecturer on Christian education, has made the provocative statement that we would do well to scrap all our Sunday schools and spend our energies organizing retreats for everybody in the congregation. Retreats, the evidence suggests, do far more to reorient people's lives than regular classes on Sunday morning. There is much truth in this observation. People are much freer of cares and responsibilities in retreat settings than they are at home, and are often more venturesome in spirit.

Some of my finest pastoral moments have been with our elders and deacons on our annual fall retreat. Not only have they been unusually absorbent for new concepts and ideas, but they have made extraordinary contributions to my own spiritual life by articulating their personal experiences in the faith and talking about what it means to be followers of Christ in our time. Some businessmen who are customarily a bit gruff or blunt in church meetings become childlike and playful when they get away from home for the weekend. Every time I have attended an officers' retreat I have come back refreshed and exhilarated for the tasks ahead of us.

Presently, the only other groups in our church who make regular retreats are the junior highs, senior highs, and one women's group that has been functioning as a sharing group for the past two years. But it is one of my dreams to see the entire church honeycombed by various retreat groups within the next few years. A new presbytery camp for which our church helped raise funds will greatly facilitate the realization of such a dream. Perhaps we shall even develop a lay retreat leader from among the various psychologists and counselors in our congregations. I know of nothing that would do more to guarantee the spiritual growth of church members.

In the meantime, we are trying to encourage as many of our people as possible to join other groups at religious campgrounds, meetings, and conventions. The ones who do invariably return filled with excitement and a new sense of commitment.

The Right Book at the Right Time

Counseling church members about personal problems and growth opportunities occurs in two ways. One is through the standard, appointment-and-visit-in-the-office method. The other is the counseling-on-the-fly method—stopping to chat in the hallway, the parking lot, the restaurant, or the shopping center. The alert pastor can do five or six times as much counseling by the second method as by the first. The trick is always to listen for little clues about what's happening in the other person's life and follow up on them, either then or later ("later" means taking the initiative to phone or visit).

Both methods often leave the pastor unsatisfied, with the feeling that he or she wasn't able to delve deeply enough or provide enough real information to truly help the counselee. What is needed is a book or an essay to put in the hands of the counselee so that the counselee can continue the search alone and then return with further questions or more feelings to share.

The library and the personal bookshelf are two of the most valuable aids I have as a pastor. I take time regularly to browse through the church library in order to keep abreast of our acquisitions, and I often purchase books I see in seminary or university bookstores or in retreat centers and bring them back to our librarian. Then when I am counseling someone and need to refer the counselee to further reading on the subject that has been discussed, I can say, "We have a good book on that in the library. I saw it there recently myself. Let's go down and check it out for you."

The personal bookshelf is even better. Shortly after arriving in my pastorate, I asked our budget committee for an annual sum with which to purchase lending and giveaway books (many that are loaned never find their way back!) to keep in my office and my secretary's office where we can simply take them down from the shelf, make a note of the borrower, and say, "Here, take this book and read it. It will throw great light on the matter we have been discussing." The book thus becomes a valuable extension of the pastor as counselor and forms the basis for future meetings when new ideas and perceptions can be discussed.

Here is a list of some of the most useful books I would recommend having for this purpose. It has been recently augmented by the suggestions of several thoughtful ministers around the country.

BASICS OF THE CHRISTIAN FAITH

Barclay, William. *The Mind of Jesus.* New York: Harper & Row, 1976.

Bauman, Edward. W. *The Life and Teaching of Jesus.* Philadelphia: Westminster Press, 1978.

Küng, Hans. *On Being a Christian.* New York: Doubleday & Co., 1976.

Lewis, C. S. *Mere Christianity.* New York: Macmillan Publishing Co., 1964.

Phillips, J. B. *Your God Is Too Small.* New York: Macmillan Publishing Co., 1964. Out of print.

Weatherhead, Leslie. *The Christian Agnostic.* Nashville: Abingdon Press, 1979

———. *The Will of God.* Nashville: Abingdon Press, 1976.

DEALING WITH DOUBT

Brown, Robert McAfee. *Is Faith Obsolete?* Philadelphia: Westminster Press, 1979.

Fosdick, Harry Emerson. *Dear Mr. Brown.* New York: Harper & Row, n.d. Out of print.

Hulme, William E. *Am I Losing My Faith?* Philadelphia: Fortress Press, 1971.

PRAYER AND SPIRITUAL LIFE

Fosdick, Harry Emerson. *The Meaning of Prayer.* Nashville: Abingdon Press, 1980.

Foster, Richard J. *Celebration of Discipline.* New York: Harper & Row, 1978.

———. *Freedom of Simplicity.* New York: Harper & Row, 1981.

Hinson, Glenn. *Seekers After Mature Faith*. Nashville: Broadman Press, 1977.

Kelsey, Morton. *The Other Side of Silence*. Ramsey, N.J.: Paulist Press, 1976.

Killinger, John. *Bread for the Wilderness, Wine for the Journey*. Waco, Tex.: Word, 1976.

———. *Prayer: The Act of Being with God*. Waco, Tex.: Word, 1982.

Laubach, Frank. *Prayer, the Mightiest Force in the World*. Old Tappan, N.J.: Fleming H. Revell Co., 1946. Out of print.

Merton, Thomas. *Contemplative Prayer*. New York: Doubleday & Co., 1971.

Nouwen, Henri. *Reaching Out: The Three Movements of the Spiritual Life*. New York: Doubleday and Co., 1975.

Oates, Wayne. *Nurturing Silence in a Noisy Heart*. New York: Doubleday and Co., 1979.

Shea, John. *The God Who Fell from Heaven*. Allen, Tex.: Argus Communications, 1979.

MARRIAGE AND DIVORCE

Achtemeier, Elizabeth. *The Committed Marriage*. Philadelphia: Westminster Press, 1976.

Atkin, Edith. *In Praise of Marriage*. New York: Vanguard Press, 1982.

Gardner, Richard A. *The Boys and Girls Book About Divorce*. New York: Bantam Books, 1971.

Peppler, Alice Stolper. *Single Again—This Time with Children*. Minneapolis, Minn.: Augsburg Publishing House, 1982.

Thatcher, Floyd, and Thatcher, Harriet. *Long Term Marriage*. Waco, Tex: Word, 1980.

CHILDREN

Dobson, James. *Dare to Discipline*. Wheaton, Ill.: Tyndale House Publishers, 1970.

———. *The Strong-Willed Child*. Wheaton, Ill.: Tyndale House Publishers, 1978.

Howard, Marion. *Did I Have a Good Time? Teenage Drinking*. New York: Continuum Publishing, 1980.

Neff, Pauline. *Tough Love: How Parents Can Deal with Drug Abuse*. Nashville: Abingdon Press, 1982.

Westerhoff, John. *Bringing Up Children in the Christian Faith*. Minneapolis, Minn.: Winston Press, 1980.

AGING AND PARENTS

Curtin, Sharon R. *Nobody Ever Died of Old Age*. Boston: Little, Brown & Co., 1973.

Gillies, John. *A Guide to Caring for and Coping with Aging Parents*. Nashville: Thomas Nelson, 1981.

Hulme, William E. *Mid-Life Crises*. Philadelphia: Westminster Press, 1980.

Lester, Andrew D., and Lester, Judith L. *Understanding Aging Parents*. Philadelphia: Westminster Press, 1980.

Levinson, Daniel J., et al. *The Seasons of a Man's Life*. New York: Ballantine Books, 1979.

Madden, Myron, and Madden, Mary Ben. *The Time of Your Life*. Nashville: Broadman Press, 1977.

Olson, Richard P. *Mid-Life: A Time to Discover, a Time to Decide*. Valley Forge, Pa.: Judson Press, 1980.

Troll, Lillian, Israel, Joan, and Israel, Kenneth, eds. *Looking Ahead: A Woman's Guide to the Problems and Joys of Growing Older*. Englewood Cliffs, N.J.: Prentice-Hall, 1977.

DEATH AND DYING

Claypool, John. *Tracks of a Fellow Struggler*. Waco, Tex.: Word, 1976.

Jackson, Edgar N. *Telling a Child About Death*. New York: E. P. Dutton, 1965.

———. *When Someone Dies*. Philadelphia: Fortress Press, 1971.

Johnson, L. D. *The Morning After Death*. Nashville: Broadman Press, 1978.

Kübler-Ross, Elisabeth. *Questions and Answers on Death and Dying*. New York: Macmillan Publishing Co., 1974.

LeShan, Eda. *Learning to Say Good-By*. New York: Avon Books, 1978.

Lewis, C. S. *A Grief Observed*. New York: Bantam Books, 1976.

Miller, William A. *When Going to Pieces Holds You Together*. Minneapolis, Minn.: Augsburg Publishing House, 1976.

Schiff, Harriet S. *The Bereaved Parent*. New York: Penguin Books, 1978.

Tuck, William P. *Facing Grief and Death*. Nashville: Broadman Press, 1975.

Westberg, Granger E. *Good Grief*. Philadelphia: Fortress Press, 1962.

MISCELLANEOUS

Bonhoeffer, Dietrich. *The Cost of Discipleship*. New York: Macmillan Publishing Co., 1963.

Hauck, Paul A. *Overcoming Depression*. Philadelphia: Westminster Press, 1973.

Kushner, Harold S. *When Bad Things Happen to Good People*. New York: Schocken Books, 1981.

Lovette, Roger. *A Faith of Our Own*. Philadelphia: Pilgrim Press, 1976.

Oates, Wayne. *Confessions of a Workaholic*. Nashville: Abingdon Press, 1978.

Osborne, Cecil. *Release from Fear and Anxiety*. Waco, Tex.: Word, 1976.

Tengbom, Mildred. *Why Waste Your Illness? Let God Use It for Growth*. Minneapolis, Minn.: Augsburg Publishing House, 1984.

Trueblood, Elton. *The Company of the Committed*. New York: Harper & Row, 1980.

In addition to Hulme's and the Lesters' books listed above, Westminster Press's other Christian Care Books, edited by Wayne Oates, are exceptionally useful. They include: *When Your Parents Divorce; When the Mental Patient Comes Home; Coping with Physical Disability; After Suicide; The Two-Career Marriage; Coping with Difficult People; For Grandparents: Wonders and Worries; Coping with Abuse in the Family; Parents of the Homosexual;* and *Parents and Discipline.*

We also keep on hand a supply of two small, pamphlet-sized books by John E. Biegert, *When Death Has Touched Your Life* (New York: Pilgrim Press, 1981), and *Looking Up While Lying Down* (New York: Pilgrim Press, 1981), the latter being a collection of prayers and readings for persons in the hospital or confined by illness. These may be ordered from the Pilgrim Press, 132 West 31st Street, New York, N.Y. 10001.

The World of Films and Cassettes

While the usefulness of good books reminds us that the linear age is not entirely over, we try also to remember that most people are more at home today with sound and visuals than with printed material. We acquire films, videos, and cassette recordings of lectures, programs, dramas, special events, and just plain happenings for use by groups and individuals.

But for the most part I must confess that the media world is one in which our church is far behind. One of my dreams is to have a media center similar to those in some universities, with facilities to broadcast on several channels into the classrooms and worship areas of the church plant. A large library of video and audio tapes would enable an attendant or attendants in the control center to assist teachers and leaders in the classrooms by showing their requested materials without leaving the center. It is a shame that churches lag so far behind in technical capabilities in an era when people watch an average of six hours of television every day, listen to tapes in their automobiles, and work with computers at home and in the office.

A sharing group in our congregation is presently working its way through a series of video tapes on the stages of life. Each tape becomes the basis for extended conversations among a dozen women who have learned to be extremely open and supportive of one another. This is an ideal usage of "the technical expansion of mental and psychological horizons." I hope we shall one day be "consoled, wired, and screened" for this kind of programming in all our groups and classes.

For the moment, we have a cassette recording library at one end of our church library, with a listening post for any one who wishes to use it. We maintain a tape copier and supply inexpensive tapes to anyone who wants to record any materials that are not protected by copyright. We also have a collection of films, filmstrips, and colored slides, and can get other audiovisuals from a presbytery office across town which acquires them for use by individual churches.

But we are looking forward to much more. A man recently asked me what he might do to memorialize his wife who had died. I suggested the purchase of a portable TV set, a VCR machine, and a small library of new video tapes. It is a small step toward the future, but it is in the right direction!

Bibles at Breakfast

We try to have a good biblical seminar, in addition to our usual Sunday Bible classes, at least once in the spring and fall. The seminar is usually taught by one of the pastors, primarily so that the biblical material can be closely applied to the personal needs of parishioners.

One of the best times for such seminars, we have found, is at breakfast. We announce that a three-, four-, or five-week seminar will begin on such-and-such a date at 7:30 A.M., with a light breakfast for participants. Juice, cereal, toast and jelly, sweet rolls, coffee, tea, and milk are available. Lecturing begins shortly after 7:30 and always concludes promptly by 8:30, so that businesspersons can be on their way to the store or office without being late.

When we attempt to teach an entire book of the Bible, as we often do, we give an overview of the book, stressing the author's intention in writing it, the style in which it is written, and anything about the time or audience that may have influenced what was said. Then we try to touch on the highlights of the book, emphasizing in each session an idea or ideas that the participants can carry away and meditate on during the day.

People seem to enjoy the format and to learn from it. They often comment on the help it gives them and the special quality it seems to have because it is held on a weekday morning, in the midst of their routines. A week seldom passes that someone doesn't ask, "What are we going to study next at our breakfast seminar?"

In my opinion, the most important thing we do in these seminars is to inculcate good habits of thinking about the Bible and its interpretation. We try to stress *an attitude of approach* as well as the material itself, so that people will learn how to read the Bible with more understanding and confidence. When we allude to various commentators and their interpretations, we try to set the commentaries themselves in at least a semi-critical light, so that the participants can see the importance of some intellectual detachment from the opinions of others and attempt to form their own judgments. We want *them* to become biblical theologians, not mere consumers of material their pastors and others have prepared!

Prayer Covenants

Three years ago, one of our elders made a little speech during a board meeting. "We talk a lot about prayer and its importance," he said, "but, if the rest of you are like me, you probably don't pray as much as you ought to. Two or three times every year, I make a resolution to pray for other people on a more regular basis, and then it slips through the cracks and I don't do it. I wonder if it wouldn't help me if we had regular prayer partners on this board and would pray for each other every day."

At the next board meeting, we distributed a list of names of board members that were grouped into threes.

"The two persons whose names are grouped with yours," we said, "are your prayer partners for the next three months. Please remember to pray for them each day, and remember that they are also praying for you."

Three months later, we took time at a meeting to talk about the results of our efforts of praying for one another. "I have felt better everyday," said one man, "knowing that I was being supported in prayer by two of you."

"My prayer partners called me," said another elder, "and said, 'We need to get together and talk about what's going on in our private lives so we can know better how to pray for one another.' So we did. We got together and talked, and I found out things I didn't know about my friends, even though I had known them for years. I recommend that all the groups get together the way we did."

"I was carried through a real crisis," said yet another elder, "by the prayers of my colleagues."

Since then, we have rotated the prayer groupings each quarter by distributing a new list as part of our board's agenda. The overall effect has been tremendous. People who did not know one another well have become better acquainted. Praying for one another has become a pathway to new spiritual depth and new personal unity among the board's membership. Even our business seems to go more smoothly and with a greater spiritual sense about it.

Now we are ready, on the basis of this experience, to suggest it to the entire church. We probably will begin it in Lent and post a copy of the church roll in the narthex. We will ask each member to note the names appearing before and after his or her own name and to remember these persons in prayer during the entire Holy Season. Then we'll shift the list and ask people to consult it again and to remember the new prayer partners for the next season of the year, and so on.

I can imagine the many small miracles of love, friendship, and renewal that will occur from this experience.

And there are even added benefits: Several board members have said, "I remember to pray for my pastor when I am praying for my other friends!"

A Ministry of Special Events

Many churches across the country have special preaching missions each year to which they invite noted preachers of their own and other denominations. Many of these missions are supported by annual grants or by the income from endowments given by wealthier members of the congregations.

As a participant in some of these missions, I have long noted the excitement and expectancy of the parishioners who await these events, especially those living in smaller towns and villages where the opportunity of hearing "celebrity preachers" is more limited than it is in metropolitan areas. Lay committees are always at work on advertising, hospitality, and program strategies. Ministers of music, choral groups, and instrumentalists are psyched up for special performances. Women's groups plan special luncheons and men's groups plan special breakfasts. Often there is even a gathering of ministers in the area, so that they have the opportunity to question and converse with the guest preacher. Preaching missions are almost always gala affairs, the equivalent in our day, I suppose, of the old revival meetings and brush-arbor meetings of days gone by.

Soon after I arrived in my present parish, therefore, I began at once to watch for an opportunity to secure such an advantage for my congregation. I prepared a formal syllabus on preaching missions, with a description of their nature, cost, and opportunities, and waited. Then, when a particularly tragic death occurred in one of our church's families, the father and mother of the man who was killed asked, "What can we do to memorialize our son in a special way?" I took a copy of the syllabus to them and suggested that they read it and pray about a preaching mission as a possibility. They studied the syllabus a few days and responded by saying that it sounded wonderful; it would be a living memorial, not only benefiting the entire community but renewing their son's name in our midst every year. The establishment of the memorial was announced and everyone was given an opportunity to contribute, with the father and mother's gift providing the majority of the sum that was needed. We formed a committee, invited a preacher, and deposited the endowment sum so it would earn interest until the following year when we would need it.

Now, each year, the preaching mission is a highlight of spiritual experience for our church and the community

[115]

around us. Other churches participate by bringing their ministers to help with liturgies and their choirs to sing anthems and their congregations to sing and pray and listen. The ministers of the area gather with us for lunch on Monday. Groups of laypersons crowd around the visiting speaker at breakfast and entertain him or her at dinner. Spirits run high, and new commitments are made. We can feel the recharging of our congregational life, as if the mission somehow enables us to get plugged in again.

Now I have two more proposals or syllabi drafted for memorial endowments. One is for a music mission and calls for bringing a musician or musicians of unusual ability to our church for a week each year to hold concerts and lift our hearts with great religious music. The other is for a famous author's mission, to bring noted Christian writers such as Madeleine L'Engle, Annie Dillard, or Frederick Buechner and let them share themselves and their craft with our people for several days. The possibilities are almost endless. One can imagine a noted theologian's mission, a great biblical scholar's mission, an outstanding educator's mission, a historian's mission, an architect's mission, a lawyer's mission, a bioethicist's mission, and on and on, interlacing the year with special opportunities for people to consider the claims of God on all of life.

In the end, this is our hope—that people will come to view life sacramentally, that their values will change to reflect the rulership of God in all their actions, that they will discover the fullness of Christ in their daily existence, and that they will joyfully set about reshaping the world as God and the Judeo-Christian tradition have always envisioned it. And we must work, as imaginatively as possible, to help them move in this direction. This, in a nutshell, is the pastoral task.

VII

Fostering a Sense of Stewardship

If we had to put a single name on everything we do in the church, that name might be stewardship. We are trying to get people to see that they have inherited the earth, including their own existence, and must learn how to care for it. All living is a form of stewardship, either good or bad. What we would like to do in the church is to provide a proper perspective on stewardship and enable people to become good stewards, not bad stewards.

Many of Jesus' parables concerned people who were poor stewards—the man who hid his talent instead of investing it (Matt. 25:14-30), the boy who squandered his father's money (Luke 15:11-32), the rich fool who was too concerned about acquiring more (Luke 12:16-20), the five maidens who forgot to provide oil for their lamps (Matt. 25:1-13), the son who failed to work in his father's field after promising to do it (Matt. 21:28-31), and the wicked tenants who refused the owner's claim on their property (Mark 12:1-11; Matt. 21:33-44; Luke 20:9-18).

Other parables clearly commended persons who were good stewards—the Samaritan who used his goods for a man who had fallen among thieves (Luke 10:30-37), a shepherd who rescued the hundredth sheep that was lost (Luke 15:3-7), a woman who swept her house until she found a coin she had lost (Luke 15:8-10), a merchant who liquidated all his holdings to buy a fabulous pearl

(Matt. 13:45-46), and the rascal steward who was suddenly shaken from lethargy and used his position to redeem himself with the master (Luke 16:1-9).

Some of the parables, such as "The Pounds" (Luke 19:12-27), "The Talents" (Matt. 25:14-30), "The Prodigal Son" (Luke 15:11-32), "The Ten Maidens" (Matt. 25:1-13), "The Two Sons" (Matt. 21:28-31), "The Unforgiving Servant" (Matt. 18:23-35), and "The Rascal Steward" (Luke 16:1-9), even turn on the obvious contrast between bad stewardship and good stewardship.

It is clear that Jesus himself saw stewardship—how we behave with our lives, our gifts, and our property—as the key issue of true discipleship.

We can hardly fail, therefore, to place stewardship at the top of our list for pastoral attention. Inculcating good stewardship attitudes and habits is necessary to real spiritual growth in our congregations.

Raising Mission Consciousness

A large part of good stewardship, as reflected in most of Jesus' parables and other teachings, has to do with what has been called "the Copernican Revolution of the soul"—that is, to get people to see that they aren't the center of the universe, but God is. When this happens, they can begin to hear the repeated word of the Bible that they are to esteem others better than themselves, provide for the poor, care for widows and orphans, feed the hungry, clothe the naked, visit the prisoners, give justice to the oppressed, show hospitality to strangers, and generally regard themselves as caretakers in the world, not owners. The service of God, in other words, issues in a ministry of love to all of God's "little ones" in the society around us.

The alert pastor will do everything he or she can to promote mission consciousness in his or her congregation—to help people think *service,* dream *service,* and enact *service* in the world. It is in learning to live for others that people discover the meaning of God's love for them.

When new members are received into our church, they are given a packet containing, among other things, a pictorial directory of church members; pamphlets about our church's programs, including its *work* and *mission* programs; *a commitment form,* for indicating where they would like to work in the church and community; and *a pledge card,* for showing how they intend to support the work of the church financially. I usually give them a little talk about getting involved in the life of the church and remind them that the church, once we have received the good news of God's grace, lives by our members giving and serving.

In the fourth and final segment of our orientation program new members hear these words from a tape recording:

It is all very well to talk about God as love and salvation as a personal experience. But we do not fully understand love and salvation until we become channels of God's blessings to other persons. Redemption is corporate as well as personal. We have our salvation with other people, not apart from them. We are faithful to Christ and we grow as individual Christians only when we are engaged in redemptive activity in the world around us. . . .

As a new church member, you should consider it part of your duty to learn all you can about the mission work of our congregation. The meetings of our Community Mission Group and National and World Mission Group are open to all church members. You do not have to be on the groups to attend. They are a good place to begin. But you should not limit your concept of mission to what our church happens to be doing at the moment. God may lay it on your heart to get us all involved in some new mission project. As a cooperative group, we find that is the way things happen for us: somebody sees a need and brings it to a larger group in the church; then, after investigation and discussion, we all become involved. The church *is* mission. That ought to be our motto. And we all ought to learn to think mission all the time.

People make happy church members, I find, as they become active and contributing members, serving the world around them. Therefore I make every effort I can, as a pastor, to help them reorient themselves toward work and mission. My associate and I planned the restructuring of our church's two major mission committees, the Community Mission Group and the National and World Mission Group. Membership was expanded to represent other aspects of the church's work, including education, youth, Women of the Church, and public relations. Each group was encouraged to develop an aggressive "sales" approach, informing the congregation of its work and its vision, and involving as many people as possible in both. Programs at fellowship dinners outlined and undergirded the church's mission outreach. Articles in the newsletter featured missionaries and medical teams supported by our budget. Our men and boys were encouraged to take an active part in a local Wood Ministry, cutting, stacking, and delivering firewood to the homes of the poor. Bulletin boards around the church plant came alive with colorful depictions of our involvement in various mission projects. "Minutes for Mission" were incorporated in our Sunday worship services, with articulate laypeople talking about the importance of missionary giving and service projects. Pastoral prayers invariably included references to the poor and hungry and neglected peoples of the world. Offertory prayers regularly alluded to the work of our missionary friends in the inner city and abroad. Paragraphs in the worship bulletin reminded worshipers of the relationship between piety and caring for others.

At the end of three years, our giving for all causes had risen almost 100 percent. More important, a climate for sharing and helping had developed. Board members began talking about "zero budgeting"—giving away all our money at the end of the year instead of stockpiling it, which had traditionally been done. A clamor arose in the congregation for more giving to missions. People began to speak of "fifty-fifty"—50 percent for use at home and 50 percent for use in other places. The more we talked about giving money away, the more there was to give away. The entire stewardship issue shifted from one of recruitment—raising a given amount to subscribe the budget—to genuine stewardship of God's gifts.

"Hands Around the Church"

As our attitude toward stewardship began to change, our Every-Member Canvass Committee began to talk new approaches to doing its work. For as long as anyone could remember, this committee, which normally consisted of men who represented the old, well-connected families of the church, had annually announced a campaign, sent out letters containing pledge cards to every church member, and then personally contacted each person who did not return a card. The system had served adequately, as the committee usually included a "tail-twister," someone who could approach more affluent members of the congregation and hit them up for additional money if the budgeted figure was not reached on the first attempt. But as we talked stewardship and individual responsibility before God it became apparent that the old system was not truly expressive of what we were trying to achieve.

We wrote to other churches and asked what they were doing to promote Christian giving. Members of our committee, as they traveled in their work, spoke with leaders in other places and asked questions about their stewardship practices. After long discussion, we decided that we liked the so-called "Pony Express" system used in some churches, which emphasized the cooperation of entire congregations in planning their financial lives for the coming year. The principal idea of "Pony Express" is to have people pass along to one another a number of "saddlebags" containing pledge cards, so that eventually all the bags reach the church office, thus relieving a few individuals from doing a lot of personal contact work. We did not, however, like the "gimmicky" nature of "Pony Express"—its use of a nonchristian name, of imitation saddlebags, of metallic seals showing a Pony Express rider, and of a generally questionable aura or ambience.

In the end, we designed a system of our own that was similar to "Pony Express" but, we felt, more suited to our congregation and the dignity of Christian stewardship. We called it "Hands Around the Church" and developed as our logo the silhouettes of people holding hands under the image of the cross. Our promotion explained what we were attempting to do. Fifty group captains were selected to monitor the progress of envelopes bearing the "Hands Around the Church" cards. Our constituency was broken down into neighborhood groups, and the names and addresses were printed on sheets affixed to the outsides of the envelopes. Inside each envelope were smaller envelopes and pledge cards for each person on the list. The group captain received the envelope, completed his or her card, sealed it in a small envelope, placed that inside the large envelope, and started the entire packet on its rounds. He or she telephoned every two or three days to check on the progress of the packet. At the end of the week, all the packets were back at the church and were brought forward and dedicated during the worship service. Instead of one hundred twenty-five names to follow up on, as there had been in previous years, there were only twenty-five this time, and most of them were people who were out of town the week of the program.

Members of the Every-Member Canvass Committee were elated. There was a good spirit in the church. They had not felt like Robin Hoods, lurking behind pledge cards to plunder church members or pressure them into giving. The congregation had caught the enthusiasm of shared responsibility. In subsequent discussions, two changes were suggested for the following year. One was to extend the time frame from one week to two weeks, to permit a more leisurely transmission of the packets in a congregation where most people are on the move. The other was to use the officers of the church to superintend the process, so that anyone who wished to ask questions about our financial life or attitudes could have them answered by a responsible person. The first change proved wise, the second unwise. Some church officers were less diligent in the oversight of their charges than the handpicked captains of the previous year. But overall the new system proved highly effective. Giving rose significantly. People began to feel more involved in the financial affairs of their church. A sense of stewardship was in the air!

"When You Die . . ."

Inevitably, as people think more and more about their Christian stewardship of money and property, they begin to develop a Christian attitude about their estate planning. Our church often received small bequests when members died, but no effort was ever made to remind the membership of the importance of remembering the church in their wills.

One evening an alert elder brought to a board meeting a pamphlet that he had picked up in another church. It was about planning for the church beyond one's death. Shouldn't we be thinking about such instructions, he asked, for our own congregation?

A three-member *ad hoc* committee was appointed—a bank manager, an investment manager, and a lawyer. They were charged with studying the options people have for "delayed" gifts, the advantages of such gifts, and the best ways of presenting their findings to our congregation. The result was a simple pamphlet reproduced on our own duplicating machine. It is 8½ x 11 inches, folded twice, making six pages.

On page 1, the front page, is a cut of our church, the church's name and address, and, over everything, the title *Remembering Your Church When You Die.*

On page 2, in script print, is the following brief introduction:

"What a comfort the church is at a time of death!"
These words, spoken by a member of our church as he watched a family entering the church building for a funeral, are true, aren't they? The circle of faith makes death not only bearable but triumphant.

Because of their love for the church, many people are now making plans to be helpful to their churches even after their deaths. This is easily accomplished through estate planning that remembers the church with gifts of stocks, bonds, cash, or other forms of property. It is a way of saying, "I am grateful to God and my church, and want my influence to continue after my death."

The following pages are devoted to answering questions people may or may not have asked about bequests to the church. On the chance that the reader may wish a guide for such a pamphlet in his or her own church, the questions and answers we used are reproduced here:

What is involved in leaving a gift to the church in my will?

It is very simple. All that is necessary is a codicil attached to your will designating the church as beneficiary to the part of your estate you wish it to have. Your lawyer can prepare this codicil.

How would the gift be used?

You could designate the use, if you wished, for either of two categories: an endowment for maintenance of church property or mission opportunities in our community and beyond. Or you could make the gift without designation, in which case the elders of the church would decide where it is most needed.

Are there any advantages to me in making such a gift?

Yes, there are definite advantages. In addition to the good feeling one receives from contributing to his or her church, there are numerous tax advantages possible from such a gift. It is even possible, for example, to set up a living trust fund that will provide an income for you and your spouse while you are living and allow the money to revert to the church when you die. Such a gift can reduce income taxes and can often actually increase income during your lifetime.

Fostering a Sense of Stewardship

Will I be shortchanging my relatives?

> Most survivors are happy that deceased relatives have left at least a small percentage of their legacy to the church. It bespeaks a relationship to the church that is often more valuable to them than the additional inheritance.

Can I leave life insurance to the church?

> You certainly can. The church can be named as a beneficiary of any portion of your insurance. Some people have actually taken out policies in which their churches are the sole beneficiaries. The premiums are tax deductible.

Are endowments bad for the church?

> On the contrary, in this age of rapidly escalating costs they provide the finest means of caring for standard budgetary needs, so that the weekly gifts of members can be applied directly to the ministry and outreach of the congregation.

Whom should I call if I want to know more about including the church in my will or in planned lifetime giving?

> You may begin by phoning the church office. Your inquiry will be directed to the pastor and to the Endowment Committee. A member of the committee will be happy to explain the benefits to you.

Our pamphlets are kept visible in a literature rack in the narthex and in the pew racks of the sanctuary. Attention is called to them on special occasions, such as our annual day for acknowledging memorial gifts.

I believe that the more people are involved in a *total* stewardship program, including their life and estate planning, the fuller and happier will be their Christian experience.

A Santa List for the Church

On a whimsical note, I turned my first Christmas "Pastor's Paragraph" in my present parish into a "Santa's List" for the church. I recalled what an exciting event writing a letter to Santa Claus had always been for our children and how helpful it had been to their parents in determining what to get them. With the end of the year approaching, I said, and the flurry some persons get in to find places to invest their money, it seemed entirely possible that some people would like to know some ways they could help the church. Then I simply offered a little list of things we needed, ranging from books and tapes for the church library to money for the annual support of a seminary intern.

Lo and behold, several people responded to the list with great excitement—including a man who had just sold his business and wanted to contribute part of his profits to an internship!

Subsequent lists were broadened to include items for our missionaries on foreign fields as well as more expensive equipment needs in our church. The largest single gift to date has been a $25,000 computer, complete with word processor, plus all the software and programming necessary to outfit us for the age of the computer. But some of the smaller gifts have afforded as much satisfaction as the larger ones.

People look upon the list as a sort of "bonus" list—*extras* they can give to God at Christmastime when they are already in a giving mood.

The Commitment Form

It is important to remember that financial stewardship is only one aspect of total Christian stewardship. We would like our people to think and feel *commitment* from the time they begin to consider joining our church's membership. When discussing membership, one of the first things mentioned, therefore, is the Commitment Form, which is a part of the New Member's Packet and an instrument designed to elicit each member's history of service, inventory of talents and abilities, and known preferences for places of service in and through our congregation. This information is of great significance in helping the new member become quickly aligned with the work and service opportunities in the church. Our secretaries and our Commitment Mission Group follow up on delinquent forms to see that they are returned to the church office within a reasonable time.

When forms are turned in by new members, they are first acknowledged in our staff meetings. The church secretary includes work preferences for each person in the minutes of the staff meeting, which in turn go to all officers and mission groups and committee chairpersons. Now that we are computerized, the information also becomes part of the data bank on each member, cross-referenced for easy printouts to the mission groups and committees.

Mission groups and committees, in turn, are constantly urged to employ the persons whose names they acquire as quickly as possible.

One church that I know of has gone a step farther to secure the active support of all their members, and I would feel remiss if I did not mention it here. The Church of the Servant (United Methodist) in Oklahoma City, where my friend Norman Neaves is the beloved pastor, has frequent "contract" opportunities as part of their worship services. People actually sign contracts, agreeing to perform certain services in the church or community for a specified length of time, and they take these contracts to the altar table as part of their gifts to God.

Teams of supervisors then oversee the fulfillment of the contracts and make regular reports to the pastors on the results of the work being done. This eliminates a great deal of the slackness in most commitment programs, for it provides for the careful oversight of all transactions and the efforts to fulfill them. The Church of the Servant is well organized with enough pastors and trained workers to undertake the constant task of review and supervision. I hope that the day will come when our church can undertake a similar program.

For pastors whose churches have never designed a commitment form of any kind, perhaps ours will serve as a place to begin.

The Tender Shepherd

COMMITMENT OPPORTUNITIES

(Please *check all* the activities in which you, at some time, would
like to share your time and talent)

Name (Please print) _____

Address _____

Telephone (Home) _____ (Office) _____

    As a committed member of this congregation, it is my desire to
participate in the life of the church as:

____ A worshiper in person   ____ A Women of the
____ A worshiper by radio   Church member
____ A church school class   ____ A Keenager
       member   ____ A vacation church
____ A youth group member   school student

In addition, I will be willing to give of my time and talent in the
following specific areas as needed:

Worship
     ____ Chancel Guild (serve on a committee of two for a period of
           one month to arrange flowers, decorate church for special
           occasions, change paraments, clean and maintain chan-
           cel equipment)
     ____ Prepare elements for Communion Service
     ____ Collate and edit Advent and Lenten materials
     ____ Sermon discussion group (discuss future themes and
           texts)

Choir
     ____ Chancel Choir (each Sunday)
     ____ Chapel Choir (9:00 A.M. service once a month)
     ____ Youth (grades 8-12)
     ____ Children's (grades 4-7)
     —— Handbell (adult)
     ____ Play an instrument (specify) _____

Usher
     ____ Sunday services
     ____ Special services
     ____ Funerals
Other   (specify) _____

Fostering a Sense of Stewardship

When Presbytery meets in this church

____ Registration host or hostess
____ Cook
____ Set tables
____ Serve meal
Other (specify) _____

Education

Education Mission Group

____ Adult division coordinator
____ Youth division coordinator
____ Elementary division coordinator

____ Preschool division coordinator
____ Family ministries task force

Church School

____ Preschool teacher
____ Elementary teacher
____ Youth teacher
____ Adult teacher

____ Aide
____ Aide
____ Aide
____ Part time

____ Substitute (specify divisions) _____
____ Operator of audiovisual equipment
____ Musical assistant
____ Arts, crafts, dance assistant (specify) _____
____ Special talents (storytelling, song leading, etc.) _____
____ Secretary

Weekday School (Volunteer)

____ Substitute teacher
____ Recreation leader
____ Arts and crafts
____ Music
____ Dance

Bible School

____ Director
____ Teacher   ____ Aide
____ Craft person
____ Recreation director
____ Musical assistant

Leadership Education

____ Teacher in worship
____ Representative to area workshop or conference

Junior Church

____ Leader
____ Assistant
____ Committee member

The Tender Shepherd

Library
____ Adult librarian

____ Assistant librarian

____ Children's librarian

____ Audiovisual librarian

____ Tape librarian

____ Book displays

____ Tending book table once a month

Newsletter
____ Reporter (news gatherer)

____ Copy rewriter

____ Layout

____ Typist

____ Production (duplicating & stapling)

____ Deliver to Odd Fellows Road Post Office

Other (specify) _____

Am presently serving as _____

Youth Mission Group
____ Advisor, jr. high

____ Advisor, sr. high

____ Advisor, college

____ Boy Scout leader

____ Girl Scout leader

____ Cub Scout leader

National & World Missions
____ Serve as member of the National & World Mission Group

____ *Special Offerings:* assist in ordering supplies, preparing publicity for newsletter, bulletin boards, and preparation of other special displays (Joy Gift, Easter Offering, Witness Season Offering)

____ *Missionary Communications:* assist in developing ways of communicating between members in our church and our missionaries and their churches in the mission field

____ *Church School Missions Education Program:* assist in preparing materials for use in our church school for systematic education in the outreach of First Church locally, nationally, and internationally

____ *Communications Program:* assist in preparing materials for newsletter, bulletin boards, and special displays designed to highlight the mission of the church

____ *Special Mission Events:* assist in planning and implementing special events designed to increase knowledge and commitment to the mission of church

____ Any other interest in national and world missions (please specify): _____

Fostering a Sense of Stewardship

Pastoral

Visitation

____ Sick and shut-ins

____ New members

____ Prospective members

____ Local cassette distribution

Transportation

____ To and from church

____ To and from doctors, hospital, etc.

Sponsorship

____ Presbyterian Home children (sit with them in church, invite to your home occasionally)

Special Opportunities

____ Assistance in homes at times of crisis

____ Housing for guest ministers, missionaries, or others

Other (specify)_____

Community

Meals on Wheels

____ Inner City Route: once every six months, accompanied by a route director

Time 1⅓ hours from pick-up at Guggenheimer Hospital

____ Rivermont Route: once a month, paired with another volunteer

Time: 1 hour from pick-up at Virginia Baptist Hospital

____ Snow Route (four-wheel drive required): limited to bad weather, no-school days when regular drivers are not expected to go out

Lynchburg Covenant Fellowship

____ Transport and accompany visually impaired to planned programs (third Sunday afternoon each month at Kum-Ba-Yah Ecumenical Center, 412 Madison St., and bowling one evening per month)

____ Kum-Ba-Yah After-School Care Program (daily for children aged 6-12 and twice weekly for teenagers)

____ Wood Ministry: gathering, cutting, and delivering wood to needy in the community—those with wood, a truck, or time to share are needed

____ Advocacy Program: provides opportunity for a one-to-one relationship with lonely and needy persons and families, primarily in the inner city

____ Furniture Exchange Program: pick-up of used furnishings from donors and delivery to the needy—those with good used furnishings, a truck, or time to share are needed. Churches/members who participate are scheduled in advance.

[131]

____ Kum-Ba-Yah Summer Camp Program: volunteers needed to drive campers from the inner city to and from camp, morning and afternoon for one- and two-week periods; scholarships can also be provided for needy children

Presbyterian Home

____ Buy and wrap Christmas gifts (list and funds supplied)

____ Tutor (1 child on a regular basis)

Transportation:

____ Camps in summer

____ Medical and dental appointments

Recreation leader:

____ After school

____ Summer

Other Opportunities

____ City Jail Ministry: possibilities for involvement are currently being explored

____ Telephone Reassurance: daily call to elderly members of First Church requesting service; a safety network for the elderly who live alone

____ Thanksgiving and Christmas Projects: assist in collecting and distributing food and other items for needy families

____ Other interests (please specify): _____

Fellowship

____ Set up tables (men and larger boys)

____ Set tables

____ Cook

____ Serve meals

____ Cashier at meals

____ Serve coffee after 11:00 o'clock morning worship on Sunday

Decorate

____ For coffees

____ For meals

Other (specify) _____

Administrative

____ Receptionist (weekdays 9:00-12:00) Specify how often __

____ Typist on call _____ at home _____ at church

____ Type sermons for duplication

____ Stuff envelopes

____ Address mail

____ Posters

Fostering a Sense of Stewardship

____ Bulletin Boards

____ Help count and deposit worship offerings Monday mornings

____ Sanctuary preparation (Bibles and hymnals in place, pencils sharp, etc.)

____ Building maintenance

____ Grounds and garden maintenance

____ Telephone chairperson to phone volunteers and schedule help as needed for stapling and assembling newsletter, stuffing envelopes, etc.

____ Responsibility for unlocking and locking church at times of special services

____ Public relations. Releases to radio/newspapers; publicize events

Women of the Church

____ Sewing

____ Bandage rolling

____ Packing and sorting clothing for mission fields

____ Cooking for freezer (casseroles to be delivered in times of crisis—cooking done at church)

Commitment

____ Tabulators (to assemble all the information from these sheets). It will be a big job and many volunteers will be needed.

*   *   *

Signature _____

Date _____

Daily Bread, Inc.

Nothing warms a pastor's heart more than seeing church members take the gospel seriously and begin using their own initiative and imagination to become involved in the mission of the church, and nothing has encouraged me more in my pastorate in Lynchburg than the formation of Daily Bread, Inc.

Daily Bread is the name of a soup kitchen that began four years ago as a gleam in the eye of an attractive young interior decorator named Leigh Giles. I was having lunch with Leigh and her husband Billy to talk about a proposal for a new program I hoped they would help finance. They would be frank, they said; the program did not greatly interest them. I hoped my disappointment did not show. "But," said Leigh, "there is something else we would like to discuss with you." And she described a burden she had been feeling for the poor and destitute of our city in a time when the national recession of the early eighties was taking a grim toll. "I would like to open a soup kitchen," she said.

I looked at Leigh in astonishment. She was such a well-dressed, well-cultivated young woman, quiet, refined, poised. She and Billy lived on the most prestigious street in the city. I could not imagine that she had ever known any poor people except maids and yardmen, and the picture of her working among the derelicts of a soup kitchen was one my mind could fashion only in caricature.

But Leigh turned out to be as tough and competent as she appeared feminine and fragile. She sold two friends on the project, and together they traveled to other cities to see how soup kitchens there were organized. They found additional volunteers from other churches in the area. Plans were drawn up, finances were projected, and a location in the inner city was chosen. Our Community Mission Group soon became involved and pledged $5,000 for the first months' operations. Leigh and her friends gave additional money and worked tirelessly preparing everything.

Among the many persons eagerly co-opted for work in the project was Tom Kirkpatrick, a man in his sixties, a former road contractor, and a member of our congregation. Tom and his partner had built hundreds of miles of roads and superhighways before the recession brought the construction industry to a halt. When there was no longer much work to do, they decided to sell their heavy equipment abroad and retire. Tom's "retirement" coincided almost exactly with Daily Bread's need for a "bouncer"—a man who could be present every day to protect the women working in the kitchen and to manage unruly people during the lunch hour. Already a deeply committed Christian, Tom began his job with the commitment of a man starting a new career. He approached merchants all over the city for donations of food, and then used his truck daily to collect what was donated. He was everywhere—in the kitchen, the dining hall, the entry way, on the front porch. He came to know by name almost every one of the men and women who came to the soup kitchen regularly, and joshed with them and patted them on the back as they entered.

Since its opening in 1982, Daily Bread, Inc. has provided tens of thousands of free lunches annually. Volunteers from thirty churches in the city have helped to prepare and serve meals and clean up afterwards. A new, permanent location has been purchased for the organization, and an open house was held for the community. Its work has been featured in newspaper spreads, and thousands of people have been inspired to see what can be done at the local level to help unfortunate citizens. It stands as a dramatic testimony to the power of the Christian gospel and as a clarion example of the meaning of total stewardship.

The Kum-Ba-Yah Association

One of the greatest advances in Christian stewardship, for many persons, is the realization that Christians can work together with members of other churches to fulfill the gospel. Accordingly, our church contributes financially to numerous community service organizations, including Meals on Wheels, a pastoral care service, and the Kum-Ba-Yah Association, and encourages our members to participate in the many facets of Kum-Ba-Yah's work.

The Kum-Ba-Yah Association, which takes its name from the African hymn ("Kum ba yah, Lord, come by here"), is an interfaith, interracial organization cosponsored by thirty-seven congregations in the city of Lynchburg, including Protestant, Catholic, and Jewish. Its stated purpose is "to participate in God's mission of liberation and reconciliation in the communities of humankind." It seeks to achieve this purpose by entering into partnership with other community agencies "to relieve distress and to improve the quality of life for individuals and families."

The work of Kum-Ba-Yah is done through a number of task forces commissioned by the association and charged with specific duties toward the fulfillment of their tasks. Any member or friend of a member of Kum-Ba-Yah may suggest a new task and the creation of a new task force. At the present time the task forces include: Advocacy Program for the Poor, After-School Care Program for Poor or Neglected Children, Physically Handicapped Program, Ministry to Deaf Persons, Kum-Ba-Yah Day Camp, Wood Ministry for the Poor, Visually Handicapped Program, Day Care for Elderly Persons, and Media Program (for disseminating information about the organization and its work).

Dozens, sometimes hundreds, of individuals throughout the community become involved in the work of each of these task forces. Several times a year, for example, approximately twenty-five people from our congregation devote a Saturday under the leadership of Mr. Leighton Dodd, a banker and a former mayor of the city, to cut, stack, and deliver cordwood to the homes of the poor and needy. And they are only one of dozens of work parties participating regularly in the Wood Ministry task force.

Our Community Mission Group works closely with Kum-Ba-Yah and strives to keep continually before our congregation information about the association and its many opportunities for service. Our members' commitment to God is not the property of our church alone; it belongs to all of God's people. And the more we can get our members involved in the service organizations of the community, the better we will all fulfill our obligations to Christian stewardship and enjoy its many personal rewards.

At the last semiannual Kum-Ba-Yah Association dinner, only a few days before writing this, the first annual Kum-Ba-Yah Award in recognition of outstanding service to the community was presented to Daily Bread, Inc., and received in Daily Bread's behalf by Mr. Tom Kirkpatrick.

Our Neighbors from Around the World

A strong component of our commitment emphasis at First Presbyterian Church has been on missions abroad, and we actively support mission work on several continents. Our own congregation, however, is primarily white and Anglo-Saxon, owing partly to our location in the community. It is extremely important to us, therefore, to have some kind of constant and ongoing connection with peoples of other ethnic backgrounds within our own city. Our connection is primarily with several Vietnamese families whom we have helped resettle in Lynchburg and with a Korean congregation that now meets regularly in our chapel.

Our most recent Vietnamese arrivals are a family of nine—a mother and eight children. The husband and father has recently been released from political imprisonment in Vietnam but has not yet been permitted to enter the U.S.. Their coming posed typical opportunities for our people to get involved in helping others. A comfortable house was located near the children's school. It was completely repainted and furnished by a committee of volunteers. Several persons familiarized themselves with information about Vietnamese culture, religion, and personal habits, in order to help with the purchase of food and the accommodation of our new friends to their acquired environment. A task force was organized to provide transportation to schools, work, music lessons, and other activities the family would become involved in.

The interaction with the large family has been wonderful, despite the obvious language barrier existing between the mother, several children, and their many American friends. At a Vietnamese New Year's celebration held at a local YWCA, with a totally Vietnamese

[137]

program and cuisine, there were at least a dozen people from our resettlement group, all wide-eyed and having an exciting time beholding the joy of two to three hundred Vietnamese conversing animatedly in their native language, conducting native dances, and toasting in their new year with California champagne! Several times I closed my eyes and imagined, from the sounds and smells around me, that I was in Ho Chi Minh City instead of right in the middle of Lynchburg, Virginia.

Our congregation's involvement with the Koreans has been minimal, because they have been self-sufficient from the first and have needed only a place to worship and have an occasional fellowship gathering. But there is something exciting about having them use our church building on Sunday afternoons. It reminds us that Christ's people are in all the world and that the interracialism is an important part of the kingdom of God.

"I need the beggar," said Martin Luther. It was Luther's characteristic way of reversing appearances in order to get at a theological truth. We need the beggar as much as he needs us. He is our complementary brother in Christ, and it is through serving him that we serve our Lord. In the same way, our people need people of other ethnic and religious backgrounds, especially those who are temporarily indisposed in the world. They help put us in touch with new values and new ways of looking at the world. And they help put us in touch with Christ, so that we are always becoming new creatures.

Belonging to Christ, being converted, means being turned inside out, so that what was once at the center of our lives is no longer there; God is now at the center. It means undergoing the Copernican Revolution of the soul. It means learning to use everything we have been given and everything we are in the service of God and God's people around the world. And no pastor is doing his or her job as leader of the flock who is not constantly working at the business of helping people to discover how to be stewards, how to be turned inside out and let their gifts flow outward to everyone around them.

VIII

Ministry in the Hospital

I like visiting in the hospital. Some ministers don't. They dislike the labyrinthine corridors, the smells of disinfectant and human excrement, the tubes and machines affixed to patients, the sight of doctors and nurses in their operating clothes, gurneys in the elevators, hothouse plants in the rooms, constant interruptions by monitoring nurses, and the sense that they are in the presence of disease, life-impairment, and death. I understand this. If one is sensitive to such things, there are better places to be. But, on the whole, hospitals are pretty wonderful institutions. The level of dedication among those who work there is extremely high. The miracles that occur in them are legion. And the level of sensibility, of awareness to life and love and value, is probably higher than one can find anywhere else in modern civilization.

People who are hospitalized are surely more open to learning about self and life and death than almost anyone else in the world. Second only to them in openness are their family members and close friends. Consequently, the hospital is a great place for ministry. In terms of Jesus' parable of the sower, the ground is never more receptive to the seed.

It is for this reason more than any other, I speculate, that seasoned ministers are generally more mature than other individuals, more stable in the presence of crisis, more wise in their sense of what matters in life. They have been privileged to live daily among their parishioners who are ill, threatened, dying, and undergoing transvaluation of their lives. One cannot move in that rarefied atmosphere and remain untouched by it. It is the minister's real "Yale College and Harvard," to appropriate Ishmael's phrase in *Moby-Dick,* where it referred to the sea and the seafarer's experiences.

This is not to say that hospital ministry is the domain of the minister alone—more about that in a later chapter. But it is a special place of ministry, constantly filled with special opportunities for pastoring.

Knowing Who Is "In"

It is hard to minister to people in the hospital when we don't know they are there. Some people slip in and out with little fanfare, either because they wish their visits to be secret or because they do not consider themselves important enough for the church to be troubled about them. Those who desire secrecy and privacy should have their desire honored, though I have found that they rarely object, if their pastor knows, to his or her dropping by to express concern. But it always bothers me for other persons to enter the hospital and return home without my knowing they were there. I feel that I have somehow failed them, or that we have missed an opportunity to share our lives and faith together during their time of crisis.

Most hospitals request church references on their patient-information forms. If people supply the references, it is easy enough to check on their presence in the hospital by phoning the hospital visitors' desk each day or by dropping by to check the church list in person. But what if the hospitalized person doesn't indicate that she is a Baptist or a Presbyterian, or doesn't specify which church she belongs to?

Part of the pastoring role at this point is to constantly encourage parishioners to help the church office know when people enter the hospital. Very few persons ever go in without at least a neighbor or a close friend knowing about it. We try to remind our people regularly, through our newsletter, our church bulletin, and from the pulpit, that they are our intelligence network, not only to keep us informed about those in the hospitals but also about those who are ill at home or are facing other personal crisis. Our doctors, nurses, and volunteer workers in the hospitals are among our most valuable sources of information. With everyone working together, we manage to know most of the time when one of our members is hospitalized, especially if his or her stay is longer than one night.

The Hospital Visit

We try to cover the hospitals each day of the week. I know this would be impossible in many cities, where the time consumed in traveling from hospital to hospital would be more than the average minister's schedule will bear, but we are fortunate to have only two hospitals in our city, each within a ten-minute drive of the other.

In my own visits, I try to remember four cardinal rules:

1. Be relaxed. Nobody needs a harried, uptight minister in his or her hospital room. Our body-language, the pacing of our speech, our generosity of spirit ought to proclaim the gospel of peace. Even when we are on a tight schedule, as we often are, we should impart to the patient an air of heavenly calm.

2. Be friendly. People should feel that we really care about seeing them, that they matter to us. I have known ministers whose stiffness and formality during hospital visits conveyed the sense that they really preferred to be elsewhere but were occupationally caught in what they happened to be doing at the moment. Most people are more ready to open up to the minister and truly share themselves in the hospital than anywhere else; it is a pity if we shut them off and don't permit the easy exchange of warmth and affection. A cheerful voice, a glad heart, and a listening ear are among the best medicines our parishioners ever get.

3. Be brief. I try to limit all my hospital visits to fifteen minutes, and often feel that some of my five-minute calls have been among my best. The secret is to be unhurried but not to dawdle, to make oneself completely available without resigning control of one's schedule. People in the hospital often tire easily, and it is not in their best interest for us to overstay our time.

4. Be helpful. We don't call on people in the hospital as a mere formality, because they're our parishioners and we're their ministers. On the contrary, we're there to assure them of love and relationship and to assist them in anyway we can. I always try to prepare for hospital visits by praying for each person as I go to the hospital and as I walk the corridors or ride the elevators. When I enter a room, I remember the symbolic value of my presence, and what it probably means to the one inside. In the conversation, I attempt to gently steer the person toward any confession of care or need that will enable us to deal with spiritual problems. And by concluding the visit with prayer, I try to summarize and point up the meaning of our visit and leave the patient with a sense of his or her being committed into the hands of God and supported by the love and prayers of the entire family of God.

A Prayer to Remember

I do not invariably pray with a person I visit in the hospital. If someone has gone in for a trivial reason and is leaving the day I see him or her, I may merely say, "I'm very glad you're going home today," and wave as I go out the door. And if the patient is a person who I suspect might be embarrassed by the minister's calling for prayer, I will sometimes forego praying. But normally I conclude a visit by saying, "Would you like for us to have prayer together before I go?" I have known only one person ever to say no.

The prayer is usually a brief one, thanking God for the care the person is receiving in the hospital and for the sense of God's presence we are able to feel there, committing the person to God for the success of the treatment, remembering the family and friends of the person, and, finally, praying for others in the same hospital. What I hope to evoke in the person is a feeling for his or her interrelationship with God and the entire Christian community, and of reliance on that relationship for strength and peace. If the person has not been a thoughtful or dutiful Christian, I also hope that the prayer, as well as the conversation we have had, will help to orient him or her to a life of greater devotion.

I have already mentioned using John E. Biegert's little booklet *Looking Up While Lying Down* as a source of helpful prayers and meditations to leave with hospital patients. Sometimes, too, if the patient is facing a serious operation or having to deal with a terminal illness, I write a personal prayer on a 4 x 6 inch card and give it to the person as a guide for praying. Here is one that was written for someone awaiting an operation:

Let your hand of loving calm be upon me, O God, bringing rest and peace into my mind and body. Bring to my remembrance the skills of my physician and his attendants, who have been prepared through the years by the gift of your Spirit. Help me to recall the history of your grace in my life—all the trials and dangers, both seen and unseen, from which you have been my Rescuer through the years. Enable me to trust you now, for you have been trustworthy in all your doings. Take away all anxiety from me and those who love me, and let us enter this experience with a sense of adventure, to learn from it how to be more obedient servants. Through him who trusted you in everything, Jesus my Lord. Amen.

People who have received these little prayers have told me afterward how meaningful they were. One woman said she took hers out and prayed it regularly once an hour for three days, and intended to take it home and pray it each day as part of her daily devotions. She had a sister who was ill in another city, she said, and wondered if I would write her a personal prayer as well.

Leaving Something Behind

Part of the psychology of the written prayer, I think, is that it often helps to leave something behind by which the patient can remember and savor the visit. There may be a kind of totemism involved, but, if there is, it is a good totemism. People in hospitals generally have a stronger sense of sacramentalism than they have at other times, and whatever the pastor leaves for them extends the sense of his or her presence in the room after the visit is ended.

If there is a particular book or tape I think will be helpful to a patient, especially one who is hospitalized for several days or longer, I try to leave that. And we are fortunate, in our church, to have a beautiful rose garden that was transferred to our property by a member who moved from the home where it was. Each year we deliver between five and six hundred bouquets to hospital patients and shut-ins. Coming from the church's own garden, they seem to carry special meaning to people, and they invariably outlast cut flowers from the florist.

When they are in the hospital, many of our members are able to listen to our Sunday worship services broadcast over a local station. For those who cannot, recordings of the service are made available to them and even a tape player is provided if one is needed.

We want to do everything we can to make people feel included in and supported by the fellowship of the church. And, as human needs are often greater when someone is hospitalized, we work harder at it at that time.

Ministering to Families

The stress of hospitalization naturally affects more than the patient. It extends to others in the patient's household, the family beyond the household, and friends at work, at school, in the church, and wherever else the patient is involved with people. These others often need ministry too, especially those who are closest emotionally to the patient. They may worry about the patient and they may also experience psychic unrest about themselves, for a great deal of transference occurs when they consider the patient's situation.

I try especially to visit the spouses, children, and parents of parishioners undergoing serious operations, experiencing heart attacks, or encountering other particularly threatening situations. It is a time of openness and reevaluation for them too, and therefore a valuable time for ministry. Seldom do we have a greater opportunity for teaching them about Christian life and faith, or for bringing them closer to the center of the congregational family.

I remember the hour I sat with a woman whose husband was undergoing a heart operation. It was not quite eight o'clock in the morning, but the waiting room was buzzing with activity. We talked about her and her husband's thirty-five-year marriage, from the poverty in the beginning to his success in business to their most recent grandchild, born only a few days before. We talked about faith and love, and the difficulty she experienced during one segment of her marriage when she learned that her husband was seeing another woman. Finally, we talked about the possibility that her husband might not come through the operation. A tear formed at the corner of her eye. "I have faced it all the way through," she said, "and am prepared for whatever happens. I realize now, as I never did when I was younger, that we both live in God. If Bill dies, we will be parted only for a while. I believe that, and I can handle it."

As I left the hospital that morning, I gave thanks for my calling. What other professional is entitled to such sharing? Who else is so privileged to enter the inner sanctums of people's lives?

"We're Glad You're Home"

Hospital ministry doesn't end with a visit in the hospital. Going home can be as traumatic for some people as entering the hospital. If they have been in the hospital

[145]

for a week or more, the experience of leaving can be very threatening. They will miss the constant attention of nurses and doctors, and are likely to feel fear, apprehension, loneliness, and depression.

Trying in a small way to offset this, our church makes a practice of sending a casserole to each home where someone has just returned from a stay in the hospital. Our Women of the Church have a task force that meets from time to time to make the casseroles; they are then put in the freezer and kept until needed. As soon as we learn that someone is home, the word is spread, and one of the women goes by to visit and to take a casserole. It is a small gesture, especially in cases where there is a good cook at home or a large family to feed. But it has been an effective way of saying, "We have followed your illness or incapacity with interest and have not forgotten you now that you are home."

We also send or take roses during the season when our rose garden is filled with blossoms. We want our people to know they are loved. They will understand the love of God much better if they feel it coming to them through their pastor and other members of the congregation.

IX

Personalizing Weddings and Funerals

The average pastor spends many hours every year conducting wedding and funeral ceremonies. This is the reason most churches have standardized services for such occasions—it saves the pastor countless hours that would otherwise be spent in preparing new ceremonies. Yet there is something unique about every person who gets married or dies, and this uniqueness deserves celebration. Often it can be acknowledged in a prayer or a foreword, or, in the case of a funeral, in a eulogy. But sometimes it seems to require acknowledgment of a more thoroughgoing kind—by a complete revision of an old service or the writing of a new one. Nothing I have done in the pastorate seems to draw more appreciation than the tailoring of a wedding or a funeral service to fit a specific occasion.

Setting the Stage for Marriage

I hate to admit it, but I have largely failed thus far as a marriage counselor. Oh, I always meet with the prospective bride and groom before a wedding. I give them a pamphlet stating our church's policies on weddings and a guideline of the steps to be followed in preparing for the ceremony. I talk to them about their personal histories and try to prepare them for certain inevitabilities in their marriage. And, above all, I discuss with them their spiritual backgrounds and the importance of their growth in the Christian faith after their marriage. But I have never felt comfortable demanding a series of counseling sessions, administering psychological tests, and probing into their sexual expectations. I fear that I am hopelessly old-fashioned about certain things, and the privacy of sexual feelings, at least until something goes wrong with them, is one of them.

Besides, the bride or the groom in almost every wedding service I celebrate lives out of the city and would find it almost impossible to attend a series of counseling sessions. Sometimes *both* parties live outside the community. My one or two counseling sessions, in such cases, are often sandwiched into the evening hours of a weekend or between services on Sunday morning.

I am not happy with this, but what can you do?

I am presently trying two thing.

One is to provide a set of counseling tapes for each couple, which they can audit on their own schedules, and some sermons I preached on "Christ and the Seasons of Marriage," and then talk with them about these when we do manage to get together. This has the definite advantage of getting them to do more by way of preparation than they were doing before, but it still strikes me as having certain glaring weaknesses.

The other thing I am trying to do is to organize a series of film-and-discussion sessions, hosted by church members who are professional counselors and therapists, that will be offered at least quarterly during the year, and possibly bimonthly. We will give each prospective couple a list of the dates and subjects for the entire year. As most of them come to us well in advance of their proposed wedding dates, they will have time to patch together a complete series by attending some sessions in one series and some in another. The couples will have individual sessions with the leaders, who will present the pastors with a summary sheet on each couple before that couple meets with a pastor for final discussion of the wedding plans. The summary sheet will flag potential strengths and weaknesses and enable the pastor to move quickly into a discussion of important issues.

The Mood of the Rehearsal

Nothing affects the character of a wedding more, I find, than the mood of the wedding rehearsal. If the members of the wedding party are flippant and rowdy at the rehearsal, the wedding itself will seem strained, superficial, unspiritual. If they are thoughtful, serious, and reverent, the wedding will have the same characteristics.

I always make it a point, therefore, to begin the rehearsal with a few remarks about the importance and sacredness of what we are doing, and then have a prayer invoking the presence of God and a sense of holiness in all our actions. There is nothing stuffy about it. Everything is said in a tone of warmth and friendliness. But the message seems to penetrate: "This is God's house and we are engaged in a sacred transaction." Even the groomsmen, who sometimes come in like refugees from *Animal House,* behave as soberly as if they were serving High Mass at St. Peter's.

An Individualized Service

There is nothing wrong with using a standardized wedding service from a church manual or from such books as Perry Biddle's *Abingdon Marriage Manual* (Nashville: Abingdon Press, 1974) or James L. Christensen's *The Minister's Service Handbook* (now out of print). There is a sense in which rituals increase in richness and profundity as they are used over and over again.

But I have found that people are especially appreciative of services that have been written particularly for them. I do not have time to write a new service for every single wedding service I conduct—occasionally, in the summer, there are two or three weddings a week. But I write new services for many of the weddings of close friends in the parish, and then share our growing file of services with other prospective wedding couples and allow them to select the services they would like to use or even the parts of services they would like to have incorporated into a new service of their own.

A few weeks ago, I performed a ceremony for two persons in their seventies. The woman had been widowed for twelve years, the man for only a few months. The ceremony was held in the woman's home, with three of her children, several of her grandchildren, and the man's daughter present. Here is the introduction to the service, with the names changed:

God said, "It is not good that the man should be alone; I will make him a helper fit for him" (Gen. 2:18). So from time immemorial man and woman have been together as helpers and companions. They are together because they would be lonely without each other; there is nothing slower than a rainy day in an empty house. They are together because they help and support each other; there is an old saying, "A man times a wife is equal to four." And they are together because the life of each is fulfilled in the other. "Lovelier would this look," said the poet W. H. Auden, "if my love were with me." God has made us so that we see and hear and feel and behave more completely in pairs than we do alone.

Thus it is good when two people who were alone, as Ralph and Wilma were, come together.

Each has already had a lifetime, yet they still have a life ahead of them. The life that lies ahead is a gift, a time of grace to be spent in love and joy. The fever of youth is gone; the delight of age remains. Yet there is always something young about love—young and innocent and beautiful. And we have all been touched by its effect on them. It has made them young and innocent and beautiful together.

Now we gather around them to celebrate in the eyes of man what has already happened for them in the eyes of God, and to join them together as husband and wife. If anyone objects to this, now is the time to speak. Otherwise he or she should remain silent forever.

Now I shall share the rationale for the introduction. Wilma's daughters were opposed to their mother's remarriage. One, in fact, did not attend the wedding.

They did not object to Ralph as the groom; they simply did not want their mother to remarry and change the balance of all their relationships. She had been alone for a dozen years, they reasoned; why should she marry now? The prologue to the wedding service, then, became an apologia, a statement of cause; and the line about having an objection, which I have never used in other weddings, seemed especially applicable here.

This is the prayer with which we concluded the service:

O God, who does not will that man or woman should be alone, but that together they should live and love and worship you, we join you and all your angels now in celebrating the marriage of Ralph and Wilma Smith. Let their days on earth be long, and yet so filled with love and excitement that each one seems too brief. Give them the joy of simple moments spent together before an open fire, over the kitchen table, walking in a shopping mall, looking at old photographs, holding hands, and giving thanks for each other. Bless their children, that they may find happiness in the new relationships that have come to them, and in their parents' happiness. And teach us all, as we have strength, to live daily in your presence, humbling ourselves before mysteries we do not understand and giving thanks for bread and home and one another. For yours is the kingdom that makes our lives worthwhile, through Jesus Christ. Amen.

The use of a personalized service was so meaningful to Ralph and Wilma that they are having the entire ceremony lettered on parchment by a calligraphist and plan to hang it on their dining room wall where they can read it every day.

Weddings in Special Seasons

Occasionally we have weddings during Advent or Eastertime. These are seasons, it seems to me, when it is especially desirable to use ceremonies blending the seasonal emphases with the language of marriage.

Here is a service designed for the marriage of a lovely young couple whose former mates had deserted them, temporarily devastating them and leaving them with two children apiece:

In the Christmas season, we celebrate the Incarnation of God in human flesh. "The Word became flesh and dwelt among us." We remember in the imagery of animals and a manger and shepherds coming from their fields what it means for God to be housed among us.

What more wonderful time could there be for a wedding, therefore, and remembering God's concern for human relationships and marriage? Carols renew our joy in the created world, and the burning of candles reminds us of God's presence in the home. The bells of Christmas become the bells of weddings, tolling out the news of God becoming man and of man and woman becoming husband and wife.

You are all welcome here as Bill and Phyllis open their hearts and tell their marriage vows to each other. It is a time of beauty and festivity, of mystery and grace. It is their time, and our time, and God's time.

Because it is God's time, and God is most important, let us pray: We lift our hearts to you, O God, for the wonder and marvel of this Advent time, and for the many reminders it brings of the birth of our Savior. We hold before you Bill and Phyllis, who are here to be joined in marriage, and their families, who will be enlarged and changed by this union. May the angels that sang over Bethlehem now sing of their wedding, rejoicing at this new bond in which your Spirit may become incarnate. We bow before you as the shepherds bowed in the lowly stable, and follow a star of love that the wise men followed. Give heavenly sanction to what we do, that the intertwining of Bill's and Phyllis' lives may bring earthly glory to your name. Amen.

Bill, do you, standing in this holy place and upheld by the affection of all these friends and loved ones, wish publicly to declare your love and esteem for Phyllis, and to be joined to her in the sacred bonds of marriage for the rest of your life, and to have that marriage blessed by the God who came among us in Jesus Christ? (*I do.*)

Phyllis, do you, standing in this holy place and upheld by the affection of all these friends. . . ? (*I do.*)

May God be in what we are about to do here, as God was in the events surrounding the birth of Jesus, and as he continued to be in the life and ministry of our Lord.

Bill, will you please repeat after me the words of your wedding vow to Phyllis: I, Bill, take you, Phyllis, to be my dearest life's companion, and engage to be your faithful husband. I promise to give every effort to the success of our marriage, and to the understanding of your needs and feelings. I will stand by you in all the seasons of our life, and in times of darkness as well as light. Your sorrows will be my sorrows, and your pleasures will be mine as well. I love you now, and I hope to love you more tomorrow, and in all the tomorrows after that. As the Child of Bethlehem grew to manhood, may God enable our caring for each other to grow to full maturity in his perfect grace and wisdom.

Phyllis, will you please repeat after me the words of your wedding vow to Bill: I, Phyllis, take you, Bill, to be my dearest life's companion, and engage to be your faithful wife. I promise to give every effort . . . .

The only rings in the Christmas legends are the "five gold rings" of the popular song. We remember, however, that the father in Jesus' story of the prodigal son bestowed upon his son a ring as a symbol of family membership, and it is entirely possible that Jesus' earthly father, Joseph, once gave him such a ring. The rings which Bill and Phyllis will now exchange are likewise symbols of family membership, of a very special kind. Bill and Phyllis, will you please hold your rings as we bless them in God's name.

These golden rings, O God, are the signs of Bill's and Phyllis' love for each other. They are gifts of the highest order, symbolizing fidelity, eternity, and relationship. Bless them now with the power to remind Bill and Phyllis always of their vows to each other, and of this special moment when they exchanged them. Let peace and love attend this couple as long as they wear these rings. Through Jesus Christ our Lord. Amen.

Bill, will you please place your ring on Phyllis' finger and repeat these words after me:

With this ring I give you my heart, and say proudly to the

world, "This is my wife, whom I cherish beyond all others, now and forever more."

Phyllis, will you please place your ring on Bill's finger and repeat these words after me:

With this ring I give you my heart, and say proudly to the world, "This is my husband, whom I cherish beyond all others, now and forever more."

Bill and Phyllis, because you have consented to belong to each other for the rest of your lives, and have given your vows before this company of friends and relatives, and have sealed your words by the giving and receiving of rings, I am happy to pronounce you husband and wife, and to declare you joined forever in the sight of God. In the spirit of the season, you may give each other a kiss.

Now let us pray:

O God, who descended to earth so long ago in the little town of Bethlehem, descend to us now, we pray, to bless this marriage. Let the spirit of Christ be upon Bill and Phyllis, that each may live humbly toward the other, while exploring the power of love to seal and transform their relationship. Grant peace and prosperity to their household, and teach them to be generous with all who live or come to live in their midst. Make them wise parents, who will impart both love and strength to their children. Bestow upon them forgiveness for all their sin and enable them to live from day to day with a sense of newness. Heal whatever wounds or scars they carry into their relationship together, and let them in turn deal gently with all others. Let the giving of gifts, so natural at Christmastime, be natural for them at other times as well, that they may be thoughtful and caring, encouraging each other in gracious ways. Make them strong in times of trouble, flexible in times of conflict, and absorbent in times of learning. Now let the bells of heaven sound with joy at the birth of the Savior and at the beginning of this marriage, that we may all celebrate with Bill and Phyllis the grace that has come into their lives. Through Jesus Christ our Lord. Amen.

A Memento of the Marriage

My secretary prepares the manuscript of each wedding ceremony on half pages in Orator type—large size, for my deteriorating eyesight—and binds it in a lovely wedding folder originally designed as a worship bulletin focusing on marriage. The folder features a Bible, a pair of wedding rings, and some flowers, all in gentle shades of yellow, green, and white.

I use this manuscript in the folder to read from at the service—it looks much nicer, I think, than a hymnal or a little black marriage manual—and then I mail it to the bride and groom after their honeymoon. It makes a wonderful keepsake, and, hopefully, enables the couple to refresh their memories of the wedding vows and prayers at frequent intervals through their married years.

The Right Note for Funerals

A similar personalizing lends an appropriate touch to funerals and memorial services. Part of my counseling method following a death is to sit down with the family members and engage with them at reminiscing about the loved one who has died. Occasionally what is recalled is heroic or unusual; more often it is the little things—particular ways of talking or behaving, bits of humor, specific occurrences that have stuck in people's minds. Then I try to weave some of these into the prayers and other parts of the service, so that the personality of the loved one is accurately and vividly recalled in what we do.

A man who has been an avid gardener will be remembered for the gifts of corn and tomatoes he brought to people's doorsteps, for the old straw hat he wore, for the time he chased a dog out of his cabbage patch and fell in the ditch, for the kindness with which he encouraged amateur gardeners with advice and tender slips of his own plants.

A woman who was a musician will be recalled through her many recitals for church and civic groups, the constant flow of music in her home, the way she taught each child to play an instrument, the time she had laryngitis and had to forego singing in a local musical, the joy she had in a particular piece by Bach or Poulenc.

Here is a prayer used in the funeral service of an

eighteen-year-old boy who died in an accident. I did not know the boy well. The references to his manners and habits all came out of conversation with his family after the death.

God of early morning and God of noonday bright; God of evening shadow and God of darkest night; we stand here at one of the darkest times some of us shall ever know, to bury a child and brother. It is dark because we are frail and human, because we cannot see beyond the veil of death and separation to the joy of the world we believe is there. Enfold us in your arms, O God, and hold us like little children. Let us cry even the tears that don't want to come. And then, O Lord, dry our eyes as you remind us of your promises of love and peace and faithfulness. Give us courage to live in a world where our dearest treasures are lost. Teach us all to see one another's value while there is time to celebrate it.

As we lay Robert's body to rest in this family resting place, we celebrate the life you gave him—the joys of his infancy with his parents and with Sue—the smiling face that will always be recalled—his love of the outdoors—his heart that knew no fear—his moments of insight into life and into himself—his delight in this particular summer—and his growing sense of adequacy and direction.

Let the faith that comforted the prophets of old and the apostles of the church now comfort us. Enable us to abide in the darkness of loss until the morning light of hope returns, loving those you have given us to love and caring for the earth as those who must also one day leave it.

Now give us peace in our hearts, O God, through Christ who loves us as his own, and in whose name Robert was baptized into the immortal fellowship prepared for all the saints. Remind us of eternity in the midst of our fleeting days and assure us with your presence in times of doubt. As Robert himself lives in Christ today, let his spirit continue to live in us, that all he meant to the world and family and friends may come to fulfillment in our own thoughts and actions, and glorify your name. Through Christ our Lord. Amen.

The references to "his delight in this particular summer" and "his growing sense of adequacy and direction" were due to some difficulties the boy had had in adjusting to school and life in general. His parents lamented that he had died just as he seemed to be getting control of his life and beginning to enjoy who he was.

A "Different" Eulogy

Sometimes the character of the person who has died will call for a eulogy, a form of funeral address that has fallen largely out of fashion in our time. If I have known the person well enough, or have been able to garner enough information from family and friends to feel comfortable about doing so, I will make a few remarks about the deceased. The object of the remarks is never to praise the person in a formal sense, but always to celebrate the peculiar qualities that made the person who he or she was in the eyes of others.

In an earlier chapter, I have mentioned my visits with Miss Eva Moore, an elderly woman who for many years was a Latin teacher in the Lynchburg schools. Miss Eva was such a "special" person to everyone who knew her that it seemed unthinkable not to say a few words to evoke her spirit in our midst during the memorial service. Here is what I said:

Miss Eva was a rare and unusual lady. To enter her home was to walk into the elegance and courtesy of the nineteenth century. She had been a teacher, and a teacher of the old school, when teachers were mistresses of their domain, when order prevailed and the English language itself was a magic spell. It was a pleasure to hear her talk of books, especially of such great English writers as Dickens and George Eliot and Anthony Trollope, or of Tolstoy, whom she reread in her last months. She didn't have much patience with television and its "thin drizzle" of plot and character. She liked heartier fare and better style. Last year at this time we discussed a recent production of Dickens' *Christmas Carol* that she had seen. "Mr. Dickens," she said, "would have turned over in his grave." Brought up in times of greater strictness and propriety, she was raised in the Bible, and her thoughts and ideas were shaped by its great passages. Her very speech, crisp and pure, was like something

[157]

from the holy pages themselves. She saw with a clear eye, spoke with an honest tongue, and loved with a pure heart. Her life was a testimony to the goodness of God and the fullness and glory of the Christian faith. Though she never married and rarely traveled, it was a full life, replete with cut glass, fresh vegetables, garden flowers, old friends, a loving family, good books, great ideas, and rich conversation. Those beautiful eyes, that were always young and luminous and inquiring, are now looking around heaven, where she is doubtless and characteristically eager to search out all there is to learn and do. She was ninety-eight years old the day she died. It was a long life, and a blessed life. And now we bless God for having kept her among us so long, and also for having received her at last in a season that was always dear to her.

The season was Christmas. Thus the language of the prayer of committal:

O Lord of mystery and shadow, who has made your way more plain to us in the Child born at Bethlehem and the Man who died on the cross, we offer our prayers of thanksgiving for the life of Miss Eva Moore, and for the many hearts and lives she touched through the years, as a child and young woman, as a teacher, as a friend and relative, and as a devout sister in Christ. We celebrate before you her wit and wisdom, her unique and vibrant way of speaking, her love of books and flowers, her gentleness with children, her kindness to all who came her way, and her absolute confidence in the faith of her fathers. Grant that the sorrow we feel at her passing from our midst may be more than offset by our recognition of her blessedness in your eternal presence. And enable us, from her example, to measure our own days upon the earth, applying ourselves to heavenly wisdom, that we may seek those things that are above, where nothing corrupts and none break through to steal. Let the grace we have experienced in Jesus Christ rest upon all of us, especially those closest to Miss Eva and those who have worked with and for her through the years and recent months, and help us pray with all sincerity the prayer our Master gave, saying, Our Father . . .

Now we commit Miss Eva's body to the earth from whence it came, knowing that her immortal soul is with God in heaven, who long ago claimed it in Jesus Christ. And unto him who brought again from the dead our Lord Jesus Christ, that great shepherd of the sheep, and is able to present all of us with him before the throne of everlasting grace, be glory in the heavens, and on all the earth at this Christmastime, for his blessed name's sake. Amen.

"I felt," said one of Miss Eva's dear friends, "that Miss Eva was right there with us in her service. I could see her brown eyes shining as you talked about her."

"Eva Moore *redivivus*," said one of her former Latin pupils. "I had the feeling that she and God were watching it all together, having a great time!"

Something to Remember It By

Family members often request copies of remarks or prayers after a funeral or memorial service. For this reason, we make a practice of tape recording all services held in our church sanctuary and giving a copy of the recording to the immediate family. We also supply copies for other persons if they request them, and copies of prayers and eulogies for all who want them.

Sometimes a person will remark even years after a service, "You know, I ran across a copy of So-and-so's funeral prayer the other day, and it was very meaningful to me. I hope you will do something like that for me when I die."

Acknowledging Memorial Gifts

People in our congregation, like those in most other places, find satisfaction in giving memorials in honor of friends and loved ones who have died. Rarely is there a death in our community without at least four or five such memorials given to our church.

Our church's business administrator sends a beautiful engraved card to acknowledge each contribution of this sort. We also print a notice of the gift in our worship bulletin the Sunday after it is received.

Many of these gifts are translated immediately into

tangible memorials—pictures, vases, urns, serving trays, tables, chairs, hymnals, and all the usual things churches generally need. Other gifts remain in a fund controlled by the Memorial Gifts Committee, to be expended when needed. It seemed to me that these were not getting enough attention. The money was simply absorbed in the general fund and, even when spent, did little to memorialize the person in whose name it was given.

Accordingly, two or three years ago we began the tradition of designating the Sunday following Christmas as Memorial Gifts Sunday, as a day to pay special honor to those who had died and to the gifts presented to the church in their honor. An insert in the bulletin that day carries a listing of all memorial gifts for the entire year, including both the names of honorees and the names of donors. Following a proper acknowledgment of the list during the service, the congregation joins in a litany of acknowledgment. Here is one such litany:

Leader: *From time immemorial, men and women have been moved to set aside certain gifts for God.*

People: They have made their offerings to temple and synagogue.

Leader: *They have bestowed their gifts upon churches.*

People: They have sent donations to the mission fields.

Leader: *They have supported colleges and seminaries.*

People: They have contributed to the work of the ministry.

Leader: *Because of their love for certain people, they have made their gifts in the names of these people.*

People: They have said, "This is a memorial to one who has died in the Lord."

Leader: *It is not that they have loved God less,*

People:	But that they have loved him more through these people.
Leader:	*Therefore today we honor these gifts and remember those in whose names they were given.*
People:	We worship God by recalling the esteem in which they were held.
Leader:	*We praise God for their lives and what they have meant to the kingdom.*
People:	We recommit ourselves to the meanings and traditions for which they stood.
Leader:	*We ask God's blessing on the continued use of all the gifts made in their names.*
People:	We offer ourselves as living sacrifices, holy and acceptable to God, which is our reasonable service.

I could be wrong, but it seems to me that this simple practice has enhanced our whole congregation's understanding of the phrase "the communion of saints," and has helped us elevate the tradition of the memorial gift from a mere habit or social obligation into a holy action that is filled with spiritual meaning for all of us.

A Christmas Eve Service for Mourners

Everyone who has lost a loved one knows that the first Christmas after the loss is the hardest season of the year to get through. Birthdays and anniversaries are also hard, but there is something about Christmas, which is invariably filled with sentiment, that makes it doubly difficult. Perhaps it is the fact that everybody is so keyed up, and that the very air seems to be full of happiness and excitement for most of the people one meets. But the first Christmas after the loss can be a real ordeal.

One Christmas I was particularly aware of this as I made my pastoral rounds. We had a couple who had lost their thirty-year-old son in a tragic car accident. A middle-aged man had lost his wife to cancer, and he and his four children were facing Christmas without the most important person in their lives. Several recently widowed women and one recently widowed man were living alone for the first time in their lives.

What could we do, I wondered, to make Christmas more bearable for them?

One of the answers, I was convinced, was a special service acknowledging their grief and trying to deal with it in the context of Christian worship. But when? The general congregation would not be in the mood for a "grief" service on a Sunday morning during Advent. Such a service would be a pure "downer" for them. So we tried Christmas Eve.

We already had two services scheduled on Christmas Eve, one at five o'clock for families with small children and another at eleven o'clock. Suppose we scheduled this service at ten. That way, anyone who wished to stay for the eleven o'clock service could do so. Perhaps he or she would work through enough Christmas grief to be able to participate in the Communion Service at eleven with a sense of triumph and celebration.

I designed the service that first year aound three themes: Words About Grief, Words About Healing, and Words About Hope. We had to begin where people were, with their sense of heaviness and loss. But we would be able to move, I hoped, to acceptance and perhaps even celebration.

We held the service in our small chapel to give it a sense of intimacy. Several elders came to lend moral support to their friends—and to me, if no one showed up. We had sent out a special letter of invitation to everyone we knew who had lost a dear one during the year, and had announced the service publicly in order to include persons from other churches who wished to join us. Approximately thirty people appeared for the service. Some whom I had expected did not come; they said afterward that it was too painful for them to consider. Others whom I did not expect showed up. A few persons came who had lost their loved ones in other years but were still experiencing grief and remorse.

Everyone who came expressed gratitude for the service and for what it meant. "It was just the bridge we needed," said the man with four children whose wife had died of cancer. "I don't think we could have had Christmas this year without it."

For readers who would like to contemplate such a service in their own churches and would like a model to follow, here is the service we used that first year.

*A Christmas Eve Service
of Readings and Prayers
for Those Who Have Lost
Loved Ones This Year*

The Call to Worship

"For everything," says the Bible, "there is a season." And for our loved ones, this year was the season of their death. Our mothers, fathers, brothers, sisters, children, aunts, uncles, cousins, grandparents, friends, left this life and entered another. God, who was invisible to them before, is now visible. Let us worship God, who is the center of their world!

Hymn: "Let All Mortal Flesh Keep Silence"

Prayer of Confession

Lord most high and holy, we bow before you as those who have been hurt and confused. We have been in despair because we could see only through a glass darkly. We have called unto you and heard only the sound of our own voices. We have lived in the valley of the shadow of death, and our eyes have not grown accustomed to the darkness. Hear our prayers for mercy, O Lord; send peace upon our troubled hearts. Bind up our brokenness and forgive our little faith. Through him who taught us to pray, saying, Our Father . . .

Gloria Patri

Words About Grief

There is no point in denying our grief. It is real. It proceeds from a real sense of loss. We know what it is to feel empty and hollow, unable to respond to the life that remains for our sorrow over the life that has gone.

[163]

The Tender Shepherd

C. S. Lewis, the great Christian apologist, has described the experience of losing his beloved wife Joy. He said he felt as if he were "concussed," or drunk; as if there were a blanket wrapped around him, so that he could neither feel nor communicate with the world outside.

"It's not true that I'm always thinking of (Joy)," he said. "Work and conversation make that impossible. But the times when I'm not are perhaps my worst. For then, though I have forgotten the reason, there is spread over everything a vague sense of wrongness, of something amiss. Like in those dreams where nothing terrible occurs—nothing that would sound even remarkable if you told it at breakfast time—but the atmosphere, the taste, of the whole thing is deadly. So with this, I see the rowan berries reddening and don't know for a moment why they, of all things, should be depressing. I hear a clock strike and some quality it always had before has gone out of the sound. What's wrong with the world to make it so flat, shabby, worn-out looking? Then I remember."[1]

Mary Louise Williams has put it this way:

"The load of grief is heavy. My body is weak, and each movement seems to take more energy than I have. My mind is numb with pain and responds so slowly to what others say to me. My spirit seems weighted down as though a great boulder rested on it, frustrating my every feeble effort to struggle from beneath it. I feel as helpless as my tiny firstborn daughter in her first week of life, unable to do more than beg for help. She lay in her bed, puckered her lips, and wailed her hunger, pain, or frustration. Did her weakness—her inability to help herself—doom her to lie there and suffer? No, her father and I lovingly and gently answered her pleas for food or comfort. I cry out in my weakness and pain hoping that someone will hear and help me."[2]

We too cry out, hoping to be heard and healed.

Hymn: "O Come, O Come, Emmanuel"

---

[1]*A Grief Observed* (New York: Bantam Books, 1976), pp. 40-41.
[2]*Sorrow Speaks* (St. Louis: Bethany Press, 1968), p. 9.

Words About Healing

Even before the coming of Emmanuel, there were good men who expected help from God for the human predicament. The Hebrew text of Job 19:25-26 is unclear, but the Revised Standard Version translates it this way:

> For I know that my Redeemer lives,
>   and at last he will stand upon the earth;
> and after my skin has been thus destroyed,
>   then without my flesh I shall see God.

The writer of the Wisdom of Solomon wrote:

> But the souls of the righteous are in the hand of God,
> and no torment will ever touch them.
> In the eyes of the foolish they seemed to have died,
> and their departure was thought to be an affliction,
> and their going from us to be their destruction;
> but they are at peace.
> For though in the sight of men they were punished,
> their hope is full of immortality.
> Having been disciplined a little, they will
>   receive great good. (Wisd. of Sol. 3:1-5*a*)

With the coming of the Savior, healing became complete. The old man Simeon, in the temple, said, "My eyes have beheld the salvation of the Lord" [paraphrase]. Wherever Christ went, people were touched and healed. Even the dead were raised from their stillness. And of course Christ himself, as Paul put it, became "the firstfruits of them that slept"—the promise of the resurrection for all believers.

It is the discipline of the Christian faith that promises healing for our terrible hurt. Robert Cameron Rogers had this in mind when he wrote the beautiful words of the famous song "The Rosary":

> The hours I spent with thee, dear heart,
>   Are as a string of pearls to me;
> I count them over—every one apart—
>   My rosary, my rosary.

[165]

The Tender Shepherd

Each hour a pearl, each pearl a prayer;
   To still the heart in absence wrung;
I tell each bead unto the end,
   And there, a cross is hung!

Oh, memories that bless and burn,
   O barren gain and bitter loss,
I kiss each bead, and strive at last to learn,
   Sweetheart, to kiss the cross.

Hymn: "Be Still, My Soul"

Words About Hope

Eventually the longed-for healing takes place and we begin to see life in a new dimension. It is not the old dimension, before our loved ones died, because their deaths have affected us deeply. It is a new dimension, a new way of being, with greater wisdom than before. Martha Hickman, a friend of mine who lost a teenage daughter when she was thrown by a horse on a family camping expedition in the Rockies, wrote these words:

" 'Somewhere along the time-line,' a friend wrote to us after the death of our daughter, 'we begin to long for the love that lies ahead.' And, in the words of another, 'The resurrection takes on meaning for us when we begin to people heaven with our loves.' Somewhere along the time-line, perhaps when one is middle-aged, perhaps sooner, perhaps later, depending on what our life experiences have given us and made us yearn for, if we are blessed with faith and hope and a speculative and adventurous mind and spirit, we begin to sense in a differently qualitative way that, while life is gorgeous, a gift of dazzling light and beauty as well as of terrible pain—and they are all bound together—and while most of us would not hurry our exit from life by one jot or one tittle, death is its own high adventure. We dare to hope in a new beginning, and that death, in that unknowable moment when it will come to us, will come as a friend."[3]

The hope to which we come is a hope born of faith in God, in simple, childlike trust in the wisdom of the Almighty. Here are the words of William O. Ecklor:

---

[3]*Love Speaks Its Voice* (Waco, Tex.: Word, 1976), p. 72.

Personalizing Weddings and Funerals

"In the economy and providence of God, it would seem unwise to prepare a universe, scatter the stars, and place the planets in their orbits; create the heat and fire of the sun, and its by-product, the wind; form the boundless deep, the islands of the sea, and the mainlands; clothe the land with vegetation, plant the flowers of the field, cover the hills with forest, and enliven the earth with song; crown the mountaintops with snow, and make fertile the valleys; divide time with darkness and light, so that brightness is the glory of the day, and darkness reveals the majesty of the night; bless the earth with sunshine, clouds, and rain, and decorate the sky with color; hide minerals and gems in secret places, and store energy beneath the surface of the earth; create man in his own image, put hope in his heart, and then snuff it out.

" 'If a man dies, shall he live again?' Yea, a thousand times yea! For a moment, he seems like a lamp that has been extinguished, but he can be relit by the hand of God to shine throughout eternity."[4]

We do not know very much about the life beyond death, into which our loved ones have entered. The Bible paints it in only a few broad strokes, and even Jesus himself said very little about it, other than to assure us that it exists and awaits us. The famous English preacher Leslie Weatherhead has speculated on why we are not told more and must be satisfied with the little we are told.

"It seems to me," he says, "that Jesus was reticent for various reasons. One is that if life after death is so amazing and men knew details of it they might be tempted to go into it by their own act before they had usefully finished life on this plane. Another is that we just haven't the capacity to understand what it is like. You can't explain what a sunset is like to a man who is born blind and remains blind. You can say, 'It's gorgeous, it's scarlet, it's crimson, it's golden,' but the words have no meaning. In the next life we shall probably have capacities for entering into a completely different form of life. We shall be on a different plane, with different dimensions and greater ranges of perception.

---

[4]First cited in L. Harold DeWolf, *Eternal Life: Why We Believe* (Philadelphia: Westminster Press, 1980), pp. 87-88. Quoted here by permission of the author.

[167]

The Tender Shepherd

"Perhaps this illustrates what I mean. When I was a young minister I had a dear friend, an Airedale dog, with which I used to go for walks. If I patted my knee and said, 'Walk, boy, walk,' he would wag his tail, jump up, bark, and be as excited as anything, because he knew what going for a walk meant. If I had said to him, 'Now boy, we will go out and sit and enjoy the sunset,' he would have expressed nothing but boredom and disappointment. In the same way, I feel that if Christ had tried to explain the next world, it would have been rather like my talking to my dog about sunsets. When Jesus talks about things that are on my plane, I can understand them and enter into them, but, to quote Him, there are 'yet many things to say to you, but you cannot bear them now. You can't understand them, you can't appreciate and enter into them.' I feel that this may explain His reticence."[5]

"Now we see through a glass, darkly," said Paul. He probably meant a reflecting glass, a primitive mirror that returned only poor images. But then, he said, in heaven we shall see face to face. No glasses, no mirrors. Face to face. We shall look on life directly and be reunited to those we love.

Prayer

O God, who has created us a little lower than the angels, yet hidden from our minds the deep secrets of life, we thank you for the hope we have in Christ Jesus; for his words of comfort and guidance; for the example of his ministry and suffering; for the gift of his life on the cross; and for his resurrection from the dead, which is the guarantee of our own everlasting life. Bless the tears we have shed and the hurt we have borne, O God; use them to deepen us in understanding and in service. Accept our gratitude for memories; for all thoughts of those we have loved and lost; for friends and loved ones who have sought to comfort us; for work to do, that is comfort in itself; for life yet to be lived, that is part of our pilgrimage from birth to death; and for our own dying, which, when it comes, will only join us further unto you and to all those who have preceded us in the journey. Help us rejoice in Christmas and its message of hope for a world in shadows. Let the

---

[5]*Life Begins at Death* (Nashville: Abingdon Press, 1969), pp. 11-12.

miracle that occurred in little Bethlehem of Judea take place again in our hearts tonight: let Christ who was born in a stable be born in us. For his name's sake. Amen.

Hymn: "O Little Town of Bethlehem"

Benediction

> "O holy Child of Bethlehem,
> Descend to us, we pray;
> Cast out our sin, and enter in,
> Be born in us today."
> Amen.

X

Ministering to Singles and Families

I considered not including this chapter at all. It is about pastoring I haven't done and programs we haven't started. Oh, we have a Prime Time group for young adults, both single and married, and our church has sponsored a Concerned Parents group to promote family life and drug-free high schools. We have the usual complement of classes and seminars on marriage and family living and communication and so on. But we aren't doing enough for singles and families in this pressure-cooker society.

It's all right to ask, "Why should the church do it all? Aren't the problems in these areas mainly societal?" In a sense, they are. They certainly cut across all lines of age, sex, race, education, and everything else. Families are in trouble today, and so are singles. It isn't an easy time in which to stay out of trouble. I know very few people who aren't living under some kind of pressure—abnormal pressure—or at least pressure that wasn't normal forty or fifty years ago.

But the church has as much right in the arena trying to help as anybody. More than most. Schools are doing all they can, from grade school to college, from private to public. They aren't responsible for the problem either; they simply have a lot of good people who want to see things improve. Organizations such as the Y and the civic clubs and the various social service groups are trying to help too. Again, it's not their fault, and the problem is too complex and amorphous for them to solve. What it comes down to is aberrations in society itself, something nobody is truly equipped to deal with.

Nobody, perhaps, but the church.

Aberrations are our business. Or, more properly speaking, they are God's business. Fixing evil. That's what it's all about. And nobody really has a clue to that but the church. If evil is ever fixed, it will be through the church.

I suppose I am a fundamentalist on that. I may disagree with the fundamentalists about other things, but on that I am in agreement. I may also disagree about how the church ought to go about fixing evil, but I do not disagree that it is the church's task to do it.

Therefore I think there is a lot we ought to be doing for singles and families to help them understand themselves and to deal with life in our time. I am frank to confess that we don't do very much in my own church. It takes the right combination of planning, personal chemistry, and time to do very much and to do it right, and we have been short on all three ingredients.

But as a pastor I am praying about it and beginning to think about it. And, with God's help, we will one day be doing much more than we are now.

I don't want to wait that long to discuss what we ought to be doing. So I am going to leap into it now, even though we don't have the programs and "road experience" to back up any of this. Maybe I will learn something important by just writing about it. If I do, it will be time well spent.

Something for Singles

What should I as a pastor be doing for singles? What should my church be doing?

Singles are not as homogeneous as the name implies. There are young singles and old singles, divorced singles and never-been-married singles, singles with children and singles without children, singles who work and singles who don't. There are singles who are Christians and singles who aren't, and singles who are conservatives and singles who are liberals.

Given this obvious heterogeneity, what are the primary needs among singles that can be met by the church? There are four such needs, as far as I can see: fellowship, resources, inspiration, and service. And because of the many differences among singles, these needs will have to be met in several different ways.

Fellowship. Most singles feel this as their most desperate need. "It is so hard to meet decent singles my age," said an attractive young woman. "If you go to a bar, everybody assumes you're an easy mark and will go to bed with them. I really need a group of young adults for social life—women as well as men." The churches that have mounted the finest singles programs, such as South Main Baptist Church in Houston, all point to the fellowship aspect of what they are providing. "We pack them in," said one minister to singles, "because they need one another. It's a lonely world out there."

In small churches or small towns, singles groups may work well as broad-spectrum groupings. But where there are many young adults in attendance, it is usually advisable to break the groupings down into subgroups to reflect certain commonalities of their own—say, a group for college students, another for divorced singles, another for widowed singles, another for older singles, and so on.

Resources. Many single adults are groping for understanding of their roles and place in society. Young singles have not lived long enough or had enough experience to be expert self-analysts or to have a lot of perspective on their own situations in life. Therefore, they will respond eagerly to programming designed to provide them with accurate and useful resources for living through the period of life they are in. "I'd love to have a support group," a young divorced mother told me recently. "I go crazy having to take care of my kids all the time, while my husband gallivants around with a girl ten years younger than I am. I'm so full of resentments! I need to have a regular group to talk to about this, to hear what they are doing to cope with similar situations, and maybe not to feel so guilty about the way I am." One can imagine other kinds of resource groups as well—groups taught by local professors of psychology or sociology, by counselors, and by older adults who have been through similar times in their lives. And, again, there should be different groupings for different kinds of singles. A young divorced man with the responsibility of his children might fit well into the kind of group that the woman above was asking for, whereas an older widow or widower might not.

Inspiration. As a pastor, I am unwilling to believe that we do anything in or through the church that does not bear a distinctive stamp on it. Merely having a group to meet in the church building casts a certain aura on it. And I further believe that the church is most helpful, in the programs it designs and operates, if it does what it does best—that is, if it injects into the planning an element of gospel-telling. This doesn't have to be an offensive, aggressive kind of witness. It can be in the form of brief devotionals at the beginning of meetings or little parables that stimulate reflection in the midst of a program or a spiritual retreat for a group that normally doesn't have devotionals or deal with explicitly religious ideas. But I would hate to think that any church had an active singles program, with dozens or even hundreds of young adults coming to the church each week, and never made a gesture of any kind to impart a new understanding of Christ and the Christ-filled life to any of the participants. It is the knowledge of Christ that leads us to personal fulfillment, and the church is failing any segment of its population for whom it does not provide imaginative spiritual guidance.

Service. It is true, as sociologists and psychologists point out, that young adults are less inclined to philanthropy and altruistic involvement than persons past middle age. But all persons grow through service to others, and we fail our young adults if we do not provide imaginative service projects that will engage them actively in behalf of other persons or groups in the community around them. In fact, their integration into the community is accelerated by such projects, and one reason service orientation is often delayed until the second half of life is that integration has not occurred before mid-life. Suppose the church were to offer all young adults the choice of several task forces on which they might serve—one to supervise a fair for handicapped children, another to spend weekends making repairs on older citizens' homes, another providing groceries for a poor family, another to clean up a local park where children play, and so on. It is easy to imagine the fellowship that would develop around the ensuing activities and the sense of worth and achievement each person involved would feel.

Last year one of our young adult classes accepted the responsibility for providing the Christmas dinner for Daily Bread, Inc., our local soup kitchen. There was great excitement as they coordinated the amounts of various foods and favors and as they planned for the serving of the meal. Several persons who were busily involved made new friends through the venture, and everyone had a great sense of satisfaction from making a sacrifice of time and effort during a busy holiday season. If life is vacuous for many young adults in our country, it is partly so because they lack meaningful involvement. The church needs to provide alternatives to the limited kinds of fellowship found at bars, roadhouses, and cocktail parties.

Enriching Marriage

Surely no pastor can help being astounded at the number of marital breakdowns he or she witnesses each year. Often they occur in marriages that appeared all but ideal. I remember a couple I was seeing in my office. "We want to get a divorce," said the wife. I couldn't believe it. They seemed to be the perfect couple—smart, attractive, well off financially, articulate and full of fun, parents of two lovely children. "Why?" I asked. They looked at each other. "We don't enjoy each other any more," she said. I waited. No one added anything. "That's it?" I asked. "Yes," said the husband, "we've just sort of drifted apart, I guess. We think life would be better for us and the children too if we agreed to part." Just like that.

Usually there's more to it—a drinking problem, fooling around, serious disagreements over money, life-style, the children, you name it. But here were two people who were simply bored with their lives and didn't know how to cure the boredom except to get a divorce.

I think the local church is going to have to take a far more active role in keeping families together. I envision quarterly seminars on marriage enrichment that will provide information resources, confrontation of problem areas, the opportunities for dialogue and counseling for any married couple willing to attend. An ongoing seminar, meeting once a week continually, would be even better. Some group has got to oppose the process of erosion, and the church is a primary candidate for the job.

There are already plenty of books, tape recordings, and video programs on marriage enrichment or renewal. And most of us have trained counselors or therapists in our congregations, or know them in other local congregations. What we have to do is discover our own commitment to the institution of marriage and get to work organizing groups and classes in which married people can participate. Some of us might even profit from such classes ourselves. I remember the statement of one friend who specializes in marriage enrichment courses: "My wife and I got into leading these courses after reluctantly attending a weekend enrichment retreat. We found out that there were areas of our lives about which we weren't communicating with each other, and that were likely to become trouble spots in the future. The experience turned us around so radically that we wanted to help other couples discover what we found."

The Tender Shepherd

Seminars for Parents and Children

If marital relationships are problematic, so are relationships between parents and children. The "generation gap," for all the ink that has been spilled over it, is still very real, and most families experience it in a negative way at some point in their lives together, usually when the children are teenagers. The incursion of TV and video in the home, the incredible mobility of youth today, the omnipresence of drugs, alcohol, and heavy sex, and the nearly unbearable pressure of peers have combined to make it almost "normal" for teenagers to rebel against their families and reflect values and life-styles antithetical to their parents' tastes and ideologies. In some cases the rebellion is rather mild and short-lived. But even then it can seem terribly disruptive in a home where the parents think they have loved their children well and feel betrayed and disappointed by the children's attitudes.

Parents are often eager for information or help in dealing with their baffling circumstances. Witness the attendance at parent-teacher nights when the programs center on "Understanding Your Child" or "Dealing with Your Child's Peer Relationships." Young people too are anxious to know more about their own drives and desires, and to understand why parents behave in demanding or autocratic ways. They flock to programs with titles like "Doping Out Your Old Man" or "What Makes Parents Think They Own Us?"

Suppose we sponsored more dialogue opportunities for parents and their children. Why not? We wouldn't have to make Mr. Jones and his teenage daughter Sherry sit down and talk to each other. We could pair off Sherry with Mr. Smith and let them talk about the problems of parents and children in general. Then, as the discussion progressed and other persons became involved, perhaps both Mr. Jones and his daughter would hear comments that would illuminate their relationship. Or we could do role-playing, with youngsters taking the part of adults discussing their children and adults taking the part of children.

And always, of course, we could try to inject the Christian understanding of personality, which is based on a theology of grace and love. This is essential, in the end, to help us get beyond mere confrontation and name-calling. If both parents and children can come to a fuller understanding of the meaning of Christ in their lives, it will illuminate their conceptions of both self and family relationship.

Listening to Children

Even apart from dialogical situations, simply being available to children is one of the important ministries of the church in our time. Childhood is not an easy time of life today. It has been suggested that it is so difficult, in fact, that today's children do not even have a childhood; they grow too quickly into the thinking and ways of adulthood. Television and preschools are partly responsible. Children now lack the great chunks of unfilled time of their own to mold their childhood, the way children once did, peopling them with imaginary creatures and using them to dream and fantasize. Initiated into sex and violence much earlier and more graphically than was once the case, they become precociously burdened with the emotional problems of adulthood. They don't realize this, of course; it is all lacking in perspective for them. But they need to be furnished perspective and helped to confide their fears and problems to persons who will aid them in understanding the world so early thrust upon them.

I should like to see us devise structures that will provide opportunities for children—even smaller children, say at the ages of four and five—to discuss with trained counselors how they see the world and themselves and to have help in interpreting situations that are doubtless confusing and threatening to them. There are therapy groups, primarily in metropolitan school systems, for deeply troubled children. Why not have similar groups, shaped by a Christian anthropology, that will provide such dialogue for average children in the local parish? Surely there could be no more responsible investment of our time and energy. Such a program would doubtless ameliorate what is now an almost impossible pastoral task as the children reach the later years of childhood and early adulthood.

Parents, I believe, would rush to bring their children to such "debriefing" sessions, for they often feel helpless to cope with their children's developing consciousness in the world of "Sesame Street" and *Star Wars*.

Recently I had a discussion with a distraught mother about her six-year-old's apparent preoccupation with the parts of the human anatomy. "He sees all this stuff on television and hears it from his friends who have seen it on television, and I don't know what to do about it. Should I keep after him or ignore it?" she asked. It was my superficial judgment that she should ignore it. But I would have felt much better if I could have responded by saying, "Your child is displaying a typical interest in what is for him novel and at least slightly forbidden. Perhaps you would like to bring him to a few sessions of Mrs. Brown's 'Listening Post' seminar. Mrs. Brown will be able to help him adjust to what he is learning and can report back to you with an analysis of his overall response to today's childhood environment."

Being There in Divorce

In Anatole Broyard's book *Men, Women, and Other Anticlimaxes* (New York: Methuen, 1980), the author has a humorous essay entitled "The Last Married Couple in Connecticut." He and his wife lie in bed at night, he says, and worry about being the only undivorced people in the entire state. All their friends have divorced. The men have gone to New York, where he imagines them joining athletic clubs and sitting in the men's bar after fifty-seven games of squash, staring into their drinks with lost eyes. Perhaps he will be the only man in a matriarchal society. He will be big brother or foster father to fifty boys. He worries about the packs of unattached women roaming the streets. Will they attack him in uncontrollable fits of passion? He and his wife confront their friends. "What seems to be the matter?" they ask.

Accusations burst out "like abscesses": "She refuses to develop a backhand." "He only likes to make love in the swimming pool." "She sneers at my driving." "He begins all his sentences with 'hopefully.' " "She won't quit shaving her armpits." "His hips are too wide." "She flirts with the dog." "He hates foreign films."

The pastor finds such humor sardonic, for he or she has heard such flimsy excuses offered seriously and knows that others of a similar nature have often been the basis of family disruption. Divorce is so rife in our society that it seems frequently to turn upon mere whims and insults.

The pain of divorce is beyond all measuring. Husbands and wives lose their dignity, their tempers, their friends, their sense of security, their comfortable routines, and, in many cases, their property. Children are often devastated, even though they manage to keep up a front. They experience guilt feelings, fear, resentment, and confusion. In many cases they are marked for life. Statistics show that they are far more prone to divorce in their own marriages than children whose parents didn't divorce.

As Broyard suggests, the phenomenon is at epidemic proportions. A school librarian recently told me that more than one-half the children at her grade school now live with single parents. When I look out at my congregation on Sunday morning, I see broken families all over the sanctuary. Often a husband is on one side with his new wife and his ex-wife is on the other side with her boy friend or new husband. The children of as many as four marriages will be divided among them.

What is the church doing to help these people? If it couldn't promote an environment of love and fulfillment so breakups do not occur, then what is it doing to respond to the victims' needs once they do occur?

[179]

I was teaching in a seminary in 1976, when the United Methodist publication *Ritual in a New Day* appeared with its chapter on "Rituals with the Divorced." "At precisely the time when individuals are most lonely and need to establish links of communication with others," said this study, "members of the Christian community know least how to respond, and the person is usually met with silence, embarrassment, and whispered conversations that end abruptly when the person enters a room." Consequently the church helps reinforce the feelings of guilt and failure that are already present in the persons, and therefore they have no means of being restored into the community or of experiencing renewal through the gospel of Christ. What is needed, concluded the study, is a liturgy—"honest, penitential, and sober in tone"—that will permit us to recognize and act out the fact of divorce, absorb the guilt, and resolve to go on together as the people of God, supporting with love and care the parties involved in the breaking up of marriage. Here is one example the study gave, for a ritual of divorce in which both spouses participate:

Officiant: Dearly beloved, we have gathered here to solemnize the end of one time in Matthew's and Anne's lives, and the beginning of another. We are so made that we cannot live in isolation from our fellow men, but neither can we live too closely joined with them. We are social beings, but also individual selves, and it is the rhythm of union and separation that enables us to live in the communion which sustains our selves, and in the solitude which nourishes our community. As it is written: [Here he reads Ecclesiastes 3:1-8, 11-14.]

Thirteen years ago, the time was right for Matthew and Anne to be joined in holy matrimony. Then they needed for their growth in grace and truth the visible bond of marriage. Now the time has come when that bond is hampering both their growth as individual persons and their common life. They have resolved, therefore, to sever the ties of their marriage, though not of their mutual love and honor, and have asked us, their friends, to witness that affirmation of their new lives, and to uphold them in their new undertakings.

Matthew Surrey, do you now relinquish your status as husband of Anne, freeing her from all claims upon and responsibilities to you except those that you willingly give to all other children of God?

Matthew: I do.

Officiant: Do you forgive her any sins she has committed against you, and do you accept her forgiveness, thus freeing her from the burdens of guilt and sterile remorse?

Matthew: I do.

Officiant: Do you release her with your love and blessing, in gratitude for the part she has played in your life, in knowledge that her part in you will never be forgotten or despised, and in faith that in separation as in union, you both are held in the grace and unity of God?

Matthew: I do.

[The same questions were asked of Anne, and she replied in the same way.]

Officiant: Matthew, what sign do you give to Anne as a token of your forgiveness and your release of her?

Matthew: Her wedding ring reconsecrated to her freedom. [He placed it on the third finger of her right hand.]

[The same questions were asked of Anne, and she replied in the same way.]

Officiant: Let us pray. Almighty and loving God, who has ordered that all seasons shall change and that human lives shall proceed by change, we ask thy blessing upon thy children who now, in their commitment to thee, have severed their commitment to each other. Send them forth in the bond of peace. When they meet, sustain them in their liberty. Keep them both reminded that thy love flows upon and through them both. Sanctify them in their lives, deaths, and resurrections, by the power of thy Holy Spirit, and for the sake of thy Son, Jesus Christ our Lord.

All: Amen.

Officiant: The peace of God which passes all understanding keep your hearts and minds in the knowledge and love of God, and the blessing of God Almighty, the Father, the Son, and the Holy Spirit, be among you and remain with you always. Go in peace.

All: In the name of the Lord. Amen.

My class had a vigorous discussion of this chapter and this particular ritual. Many students felt that it is wrong for the church even to appear to condone divorce by gracing it with such liturgical recognition. Others argued that the church must not be like an ostrich, with its head in the sand, pretending not to take notice of the personal and private disasters of its members.

Whatever one's viewpoint about the use of an actual ritual for divorce, it is clear that we should do everything we can to minister to the unfortunate victims of divorce. Classes bearing such titles as "So You're Thinking About Divorce?" "What Do You Do When You Wake Up Alone?" "So Your Parents Are Divorced," "His, Hers, and Ours—Dealing with the Children of Divorce," and "Divorce: Making the Best of a Bad Mess" should abound in our churches. Support groups geared to single men, single women, and children of divorce should be readily available. Specially trained visitors bearing literature on divorce and information about the church's program should call on affected persons even before the divorce occurs, if possible. Sermons on Christian love and its applications to the question of divorce should be heard from the pulpit. The entire church should be sensitively tuned to the needs of newly divorced persons and their children, so that the community of friends will be strongest precisely when it is needed, instead of appearing to fade away under the pressure of events.

Perhaps your church has already found its way in these difficult matters. Ours hasn't. But, as I said at the beginning of the chapter, the needs are apparent, and we are beginning to think about them. I hope we shall soon be able to report a better pastoral stewardship in them.

XI

Turning Sheep into Shepherds

"I wish I were ten men," said a pastor recently. "If I were, I could get something done in this parish. As it is, I always feel that I'm three steps behind and two steps sideways, trying to keep up with all there is to do."

I sympathize. There is a lot to do in every parish, however small it is.

But there is an answer. It is to turn other people into pastors. Not ordained pastors, of course. That would take more doing than we're qualified for. But effective shepherds of the flock. That we can do, with some skill, some work, and some prayer.

I have always liked the sign I've seen on a lot of churches. It says: "John Q. Cleric, Pastor; All the members, Ministers." That is the idea—turning everybody into a minister, so that the work of pastoring gets done on a large scale.

This has two advantages. One, it gets the pastoring done, and, two, it greatly deepens the spiritual lives of those who help us.

It is a true saying, "If you want to learn something, teach it." It is similarly true that those who engage in pastoring with us learn more about the Christian faith than anyone else. As they minister to others, either in the normal course of events or in crisis, they discover how relevant the gospel is to their own lives.

Ideally, therefore, we ought to turn every new

Christian into a pastor. There would be no better
indoctrination into the faith, no surer guarantee of a life
of genuine commitment. The entire church would be
honeycombed with little pastorates, and every member
would find fulfillment in learning and growing while
serving other members. Nobody would have time to
complain about anything. The whole pastorate would be
alive with the exchange of gifts and caring.

A Design for Pastoring

In fact, it is almost impossible to turn every church
member into a pastor. Many people are far more oriented
to taking from others than to giving to them. It is
necessary therefore for the real pastor to be always
working at the task of turning sheep into shepherds and
of finding strategies for the accomplishing of this bit of
pastoral legerdemain.

I spent nearly two years working at a suitable plan for
our church, and those who have cooperated in making
the plan work have spent another two years in rough
adjustments and fine tuning.

We began with our church officers, approximately fifty
elders and deacons. On entering office, each of these
officers takes an oath to give spiritual and physical
oversight to the people of God in our congregation by
visiting the sick, comforting the bereaved, caring for the
poor, and generally "being there" for any person in
distress or need. Some are naturally serious about their
commitment to the office and will move heaven and earth
to accomplish what they have promised to do. Others,
without actually meaning to fail in their obligations,
simply don't get around to doing what they know they
ought to do. We wanted to give them a framework for
their duties of oversight—something that would guide
them in the easy fulfillment of their good intentions.

So we started by dividing the work of "general
pastoring"—the pastoring not done by the professional
pastors themselves—into several categories of need, and
then appointing the officers as "lead" members of teams

designed to serve the needs. Each officer would in turn select one other church member to serve with him or her on the team. In this way we would involve approximately one hundred people in a ministry of pastoral visitation and care.

Here is the general outline with which we began:

A VISITATION PROGRAM FOR
FIRST PRESBYTERIAN CHURCH

1. *For the Sick*
Teams of two persons, composed of one officer and one non-officer of the officer's selection, to visit each hospitalized member during the course of one week every six weeks. That is, each team will be "on" one week, "off" five weeks, then "on" again.

2. *For the Shut-Ins*
Teams of two persons, composed of one officer and one non-officer of the officer's selection, visiting all shut-ins once a month. Each team will be assigned only one or two shut-ins, and will visit these each month.

3. *For Absentees and MIAs (persons "missing in action")*
One team, composed of a captain who is an officer plus four non-officers to be chosen by the captain in consultation with the pastor or associate pastor, telephoning and/or visiting church members who have not been in attendance for three or four weeks. The team will meet monthly to share notes on absentees and make assignments to individual team members to contact them.

4. *For the Bereaved*
One team, composed of a captain who is an officer plus one other officer and three non-officers to be chosen by the captain in consultation with the pastor or associate pastor, from which two members will be assigned to each individual or family in the church that suffers the loss of a loved one. The two-member subteam will personally call on the individual or family four times: at the time of the bereavement, during the week following the funeral or memorial service, one month later, and on the anniversary of the death.

5. *For Persons in Crisis*
One team, composed of two officers, to contact, either individually or together, persons known to be undergoing

extreme personal stress from such causes as the illness of a relative, the loss of a job, or some unusual domestic or economic hardship. The team may recruit others to assist them in specific instances where such help is deemed useful.

6. *For Prospective Members*
Teams of two persons, composed of an officer and a non-officer of the officer's choice, to call on prospective members with information about the Christian faith, the Presbyterian Church, U.S.A., and First Presbyterian Church of Lynchburg. There will be six teams, each serving a month every six months. A permanent coordinator will keep records of all contacts and receive suggestions from the church membership about persons considered prospects.

7. *For New Members*
One officer each month to telephone all new members for that month. Also, in cases of new members who have been contacted as prospective members, the contacting team to telephone those particular new members.

The general chairperson selected to head the pastoral program was a bank officer who had formerly been a minister. My associate minister became the staff liaison officer to work directly with the chairperson and provide supervision and detailed assistance.

As in everything, we found that those divisions of the program worked well that had resourceful, committed chairpersons at the head of them. The teams for the sick, the shut-ins, absentees or Mias, and new members worked exceptionally well. So did the team for persons in crisis, which, although it was called into action only occasionally, distinguished itself by providing helpful, prayerful relief to persons in more-or-less catastrophic situations. The least effective teams were the ones for the bereaved and for prospective members.

Work with the bereaved, we discovered, was very unsettling to the persons charged with that duty. They found it unnatural to visit people whom they had not known well before a crisis occurred and eventually defaulted on the assignment, preferring to let the professional pastors handle it.

And, curiously enough, those assigned to visit prospective church members likewise found it awkward to call on people with whom they did not already have a working acquaintance. This seemed strange to me, for several of the persons working this unit of the program were crack salespeople accustomed to calling on strangers in their business.

Eventually, in consultation with the chairperson of the entire program and the chairperson of the prospective member division, we decided to remove this subgrouping altogether and assign its work to the Evangelism Mission Group of the church, which had not been in existence when the program began.

Now, after more than two years of operation, the pastoral program is operating with reasonable efficiency and helpfulness. It has not taken the place of the professional pastors and their work, and was not intended to. But it has supplemented the work of the professionals, sometimes dramatically, and gives us great satisfaction by providing serious places of service for our officers and many other responsible church members.

Recently, for example, a young woman in our parish attempted to take her own life. Her father had died a few weeks earlier, and then her boy friend had told her he didn't wish to marry her. Depressed, friendless, and without funds, she overdosed on pills and wound up in the detention ward of the psychiatric unit. While the pastors of the church called on her regularly and monitored her progress, it was really the chairperson of the crisis unit of our pastoral program who did the most to care for her in her extreme condition. He investigated her financial situation, arranged for her to receive a month-long program in rehabilitation from drug abuse (his investigation turned up her history as an abuser), gave her extensive advice on the management of her affairs, and became her confidant in her emotional problems as well.

Earlier, this same person had responded to the

financial needs of an older couple who had been ill. He became a good friend to the couple and occasionally supported them with gifts out of his own pocket. At Christmas, he purchased a lovely robe for the woman (her husband was hospitalized with a stroke), which he had gift-wrapped and took to her home. She wept when she opened it and said it was the first time in years she had had a present of any kind.

If this had been the only thing to come out of it, the whole program would have been an overwhelming success. It was, of course, only one small story out of many about the contributions of our lay "pastors."

Hints for Helpful Visitation

For a part of our training of church officers and others who go into homes, offices, and hospital rooms to carry on our pastoral visitation program, I drew up a little booklet of twenty suggestions to relieve anxiety and, I hope, to make the visits meaningful. The cover of the booklet bears a picture of the church and the title "Hints for Helpful Visitation." Inside the front cover is a prayer:

Lord, it is a privilege to visit in your name. People need my presence as testimony to your love, and being with them enriches my life as well. Thank you for the opportunity. Amen.

The back cover bears a scriptural quotation: "Truly I say to you, as you did it to one of the least of these . . . you did it to me" (Matt. 25:40).

The other five pages bear the twenty suggestions, with lots of white space around them and some appropriate pictures or line drawings. Here, for anyone who could like to use them, are the suggestions:

1.

Presence is the most important thing you have to give. In a world as busy and impersonal as ours, your being there will mean a lot.

2.

Any verbalization should be simple and natural. You are not trying to sell anything, and should not feel the compulsion to be articulate and persuasive.

3.

Touch people if it seems comfortable to do so. A warm handshake or a pat on the back can be very meaningful, for example, to lonely shut-ins or persons who have recently moved. An arm on the shoulder or an embrace speaks volumes to those in grief or crisis.

4.

Tears are okay. If you feel moved by someone's misfortune or loss, let yourself cry. It will be remembered with affection.

5.

When visiting a person in the hospital, don't turn the conversation to your own experiences with illness. You may mention them for purposes of identification, but don't focus on them. Similarly, when visiting where there is grief or crisis, don't rehearse your own losses or problems unless to do so appears helpful.

6.

Go at a time that will be convenient or meaningful to those you visit. Observe the visiting hours in hospitals.

7.

It is generally best to arrange appointments with people you visit unless they are in the hospital. Always keep appointments or phone if prevented from doing so. Be reasonably punctual.

8.

Visits should be long enough to be meaningful and short enough to be sensible. Don't overstay your welcome.

9.

Try to eliminate distractions that interfere with your visit. For example, say, "My hearing is not as good as it was. Would you mind if I turned down the TV for a minute?"

10.

In all visits, convey an attitude of cordiality and sympathy. Be positive, not negative. If you can't say an affirmative word, bite your tongue.

11.

Do not permit yourself to be drawn into pointless criticism or gossip.

12.

Do not let yourself be lured into ecclesiastical or doctrinal arguments. Remember that "comparisons are odious," especially when you are a visitor!

13.

Try not to seem "churchy" or pietistic. This embarrasses people. Relax and be yourself. It may be best not to carry a Bible or go in your best clothes.

14.

Pray with people only when they request it or you feel comfortable offering to pray with them.

15.

Leave behind some physical reminder of your visit—flowers, a card, a pamphlet, a church bulletin, a newsletter, a sermon, or a book.

16.

Offer any helpful service you can render to those you visit—and be sure to perform it!

17.

Follow up your visit, whenever possible, with further contact—a note, a telephone call, an act of kindness.

18.

Remember that you go in the power of God's Spirit, and that the results are in God's hands, not yours. You cannot know the full extent of what you are doing for people.

19.

Have a brief prayer, silent or spoken, before the visit. This sets your own heart in the proper context for what you are doing.

20.

Make those you visit part of your prayer life after visiting them. Continue to remember them and be concerned for them. Then the phrase "the communion of saints" will have real meaning for you.

I try to review the booklet periodically with new officers and others involved in the pastoral program, expanding briefly on each of the suggestions. This seems to reduce their anxieties and bolster their courage as they enter the program, for most of the suggestions are geared to reminding them of only two things: be natural, for God is with you.

In addition, we schedule an occasional day of lectures on lay-pastoral care by qualified counselors or therapists, so that those who are growing in pastoral ministry may deepen their understanding of this vital area of service. When Dr. William Oglesby spent a day with us discussing ministry to the dying and their families, several of our officers said they felt 100 percent more prepared to take on this kind of ministry, and, moreover, that they themselves were much less frightened of dying.

Group Leaders Galore

At a crucial point in my own life of faith, I happened to all in with some people who, for one reason or another in their pilgrimages, were seeking a new experience of a religious nature. We formed a small group that met regularly each week for approximately seven months. Although this was before the great popularity of small groups and before any of us had ever heard of the work that had been done at the National Training Laboratories in Bethel, Maine, we stumbled along toward many of the central tenets of group life, discovering them more by trial and error than by actual plan. At this point in my life, the group experience became my salvation. It helped me to reclaim my faith in new dimensions, provided a cadre of friends who are still dear to me, and resulted in my publishing a book called *All You Lonely People/All You Lovely People,* now long out of print.

When I came to my pastorate, I knew that one of my priorities would be to establish a network of small groups, a honeycombing of the congregation with intimate structures to provide "enfleshing" opportunities for the people's faith. I had read Robert Raines' *New Life in the Church* (New York: Harper & Row, 1980) and Clyde Reid's *Groups Alive, Church Alive* (1969; now out of print) and was in full agreement with their premise that true spiritual renewal can enter the life of a large congregation more readily through cell groups than by any other means.

Accordingly, at the end of a year of getting established, learning routines, and acquiring some personal knowledge of the people in my congregation, I drafted a list of more than forty persons whom I thought capable of leading a group and sent them the following letter:

Dear So-and-So,

I would like to invite you to become part of a group leadership training seminar that I plan to conduct on Sunday evenings in January and February. It is my conviction that a healthy church, especially if it is a large one, needs a lot of small groups that permit people to get to know one another and share their faith and problems. But small groups do not just happen. They require leaders. Leadership is not difficult. It does not mean getting up in front of people and making talks or anything like that. But it does mean knowing a few principles of group dynamics and how to help a group go about its business.

I am inviting you, along with approximately forty other persons, to be part of a training lab and then, if you feel that you can do it, to let us make you the nucleus for a small group that would meet weekly for three months after that. I am asking so many people because I know that some will be unable to make the commitment at this time. If that is true in your case, I will certainly understand. But I believe it will be a rewarding time to all if you are able to be part of the seminar.

My plan is that we shall meet each Sunday evening, beginning January 3, from 7:30 to 9:30. The first forty-five minutes will be spent in an informal lecture format, so that we can share some research about groups and group techniques. For the remainder of the time, we shall break into small groups and participate in some sharing exercises, actually experiencing what it is to be part of a group. Out of this seminar experience I expect us to be able to offer several kinds of small groups to our congregation: simple sharing groups, therapy groups, grief groups, Bible study groups, prayer groups, special interest groups.

Prayerfully, please consider responding affirmatively to this invitation. I think you will be very glad you did. And don't feel that it is something you can't do. There is no performance standard to be met; everything is based on who you are and what you feel comfortable with. There is only one hitch: for continuity's sake, the group would need your time commitment for the entire schedule of meetings.

Hopefully yours,

John Killinger

To my delight, twenty-five agreed to commit themselves for the entire two months of sessions. And, as a matter of fact, we extended our meetings into March, so that we had a total of ten Sunday evenings together.

Each Sunday evening, I spent forty-five minutes reviewing general principles of communication and group life, as drawn from my own experience and from the works of Carl Rogers, Clyde Reid, Thomas C. Oden, and numerous other writers. Then we divided into three small groups for personal sharing, with instructions to watch particularly for the principles enunciated at the earlier session that night.

The groups worked fantastically! Almost everyone reported a sense of great intimacy in the groups and a true spirit of sharing. Several persons going through times of personal crisis said they were tremendously helped, and could hardly wait for the week to pass so they could come back to their group settings. One man said, "I had no idea I could really share my faith as I have, but, as I have listened to the agonies of others being revealed in the group, I have felt compelled to come forth with whatever I had that might help."

I was rubbing my hands and dreaming of what our church was going to be like in a few months, after these twenty-five persons were the leaders of twenty-five different groups in the congregation!

Then the end of the seminar arrived. Most of the participants expressed sorrow that it was over. I asked how many of them were then willing to become the linchpins for new groups to be formed in the congregation. No one volunteered. In the meantime, we had asked the congregation to respond to a questionnaire about the kind of group each member would like to belong to. A handful of persons said they would like to be in a Bible study group. To borrow a line from J. B. Priestley, "I felt like a man who had quietly arranged a show of etchings in a Home for the Blind." The time was not right. I had not properly prepared the congregation with a vision of what we might accomplish.

But the story has a happy ending. I have been observing, these past two or three years, the persons who spent the ten weeks in the seminar on groups. Almost to a person, they have become instrumental in the life of the church. As Sunday school teachers, youth leaders, officers of the church, opinion formers, they have quietly assumed positions of leadership. They are leavening the whole congregation with their ability to listen, to probe, to share, and to provide the right kind of group dynamic.

A very important women's sharing group has developed almost spontaneously in the church, and there are hints from others desiring similar groups. The time is ripening, and the leaders are available. One showed up in the ranks of the women's group. I am now taking soundings. I anticipate that we shall be forming two or three groups shortly. Then others shall come. Who knows? Maybe the only thing wrong was my timetable. Perhaps the church will one day be honeycombed by groups after all, and the shepherds are even now out there milling around, looking for their sheep.

Developing Evangelism

Our church could hardly be called an evangelistic church. With all the major committees or task forces that formed the structural life of our congregation when I arrived, there was not even one devoted to the work of evangelism. Visitation and the cultivation of new members were left largely to the minister and one or two faithful officers. Evangelism seemed, in fact, to have unwelcome connotations. It was almost as if it belonged to an element of society and the church unacceptable to our people.

What was at work, I think, was an inaccurate and unhealthy picture of evangelism, one associating it with coercive methods and opportunistic preachers. I slowly set about trying to change this by preaching about conversion as a process of the Christian life and talking about evangelism as the major task of the church. "Evangelism," I said in as many ways as I could, "is helping people appropriate the Good News of God's love in any way that will save and enrich their lives. It does not always accomplish its work instantly or dramatically. Sometimes it is the work of years. But no church is being the church that does not see evangelism as its primary reason for existence."

Eventually the time came for our staff to make some recommendations to the board of elders for some changes and additions to our mission-group structure. One of the additions we recommended was an Evangelism Mission Group, to be charged with continually fostering a spirit of evangelism in our church and overseeing a program of outreach to the unconverted and unchurched in our area of the community. The recommendation was accepted and a dozen men and women were appointed to serve on the Mission Group.

Our first act as a Mission Group (I say "our" because I was the staff liaison person for the group) was to engage in a thorough study of George E. Sweazey's book *The Church as Evangelist* (New York: Harper & Row, 1978). The book was a wise choice. Balanced, compassionate, witty, and well-written, it became a neutral ground for both skeptical and "born-again" persons on the Mission Group. We spent six months with the book, giving each member time to voice opinions about everything in it. By the time we had completed our study, we were a unified committee, all convinced of the need to approach evangelism as a priority for our church.

"Why don't we get Dr. Sweazey to come to our church and speak to us?" someone suggested. So we did. We had an Evangelism Weekend. On Friday night we had a dinner with Dr. Sweazey as the speaker. Saturday morning we had a workshop on evangelism, with role-playing and discussion, all directed by Dr. Sweazey. And on Sunday morning, Dr. Sweazey preached on evangelism at both of our worship services. He did a magnificent job. Urbane, gentle, yet unswerving in his commitment, he convinced even the skeptics that the church does indeed have an obligation to play the evangelist in our society.

The next step, as Dr. Sweazey suggested, was to enlarge our Mission Group to include representatives of every important area of the church's life—the church school, the youth groups, the Women of the Church, the young adults, and the Keenagers. This we did. And we took the second step, acquiring "the little wooden box," or file of prospects, Dr. Sweazey insists on as the most important piece of furniture in the church. We didn't have a wooden box, but we had lists of prospects developed primarily from the Friendship Books we were using in our worship services.

At last we were ready to launch out into the deep. We announced a visitation effort to coincide with a Fellowship Dinner. The Mission Group members, plus others who were willing to join us, met briefly for assignments which were typed on 3" x 5" cards, broke into pairs, and went out to call in the homes of prospective members. Then we came back to the church for a debriefing.

Only two persons joined the church as a result of that first visitation effort. But the important thing was that the old pattern of inaction was broken. Members of our congregation had actually met and gone out to be evangelists in our community. Now the visitation is a monthly event. It is nothing to write up for a magazine on evangelism. But it is a vital aspect of our church's ministry and our congregation's way of regarding itself. Slowly the image of evangelistic isolation is being eroded and a new image of ourselves is forming.

Now people say, "It isn't the minister's responsibility to go out and bring people into the church, it is ours." For a sophisticated congregation like ours, that is a great admission. It is an important step toward the day when all of the sheep will become shepherds, caring for God's children who haven't been brought into the fold.

A Continual Emphasis on Love

Something has been happening to me lately. I think I am beginning to understand what it means to love. Oh, I have talked about love for many years now, and I have professed to understand it before. But now I am really beginning to see into its mystery.

It is a feeling I have been getting from the pastorate. It is a feeling of acceptance, of belonging, of everything's being okay. I felt it when I first heard the gospel, when I first felt that God's love for me was overwhelming everything else in my life—all the pain and humiliation and defeat of my earlier years. Then I sort of lost it in all those years of struggling to get an education and make a mark in the world and have a family and raise them properly. Now it is back again. Only it is stronger and better than before. Now I recognize it with more maturity, and know what it is.

It is the love of God, lapping at the shores of my life like an ocean, wanting to overrun me, swallow me up, carry me off forever.

It is a wonderful feeling, and I want others to have it too. I want everybody in my parish to have it.

It is all so clear to me now. If only they could see it. But that is my job, to help them see it. It simplifies everything to know this. All I have to do is help them see it, to know that God loves them, that God is trying to overtake all of us in love.

If only everybody would stop struggling and let it happen.

But people can't help struggling if they don't know. That is why I have to help them. I have to help them know. And that defines the whole burden of the ministry. It isn't just preaching and teaching and organizing committees and carrying food to the poor; it's helping them know that God loves them.

Realizing this makes a difference in everything I do. It means that all the programming has to do with making love more real, more attainable, in their lives. It means that all the preaching begins and ends in love. It means that all the praying and all the building have but one goal in mind: drawing everyone into the love.

I know this sound simplistic, but it's true. Love is the object of everything in the parish.

Pastoring is so much easier when one sees this. Then there is no sweat about anything. You just keep loving and being loved, being loved and loving. You talk about love, you share love, you eat and drink love at the Lord's Table. When anyone, out of exhaustion or misunderstanding or anxiety, treats you any way but lovingly, you respond with love and forgiveness. And, in the end, nothing can stand before love. It is going to win the world, because God is love and God is going to overcome everything. All you have to do is accept this and enjoy it.

Turning Sheep into Shepherds

Turning sheep into shepherds is not very hard when you think of it this way. It is loving them until they are ready to share the love too—until they can't help sharing it because it is filling their lives and running over and has to go somewhere. That's what I see in my sheep who have become shepherds. They finally let go and joined the irresistible movement of love. It was like a small flood they couldn't fight anymore, so they relaxed and flowed with it, and now they are having a good time loving other people. Eventually, the other people will be shepherds too. That's the way it works. We will all be shepherds to one another, sharing the love.

A Prayer for All of Us

O God who loves us when we are at our worst—when we have broken the rules of life, when we have injured our health, when we have mistreated our friends and families, when we have hated ourselves and complained about you—teach us how to love with your love. Let us begin by caring for ourselves—for our health, for our spirits, for our welfare and our joy. Then, out of the fullness of the self, let us reach out to others, caring for *their* health and spirits and welfare and joy. Show us how the death and resurrection of Christ are related to all of this—to forgiveness of our sins and fullness of life and the desire to follow him by giving ourselves for others. And grant, O God, that, leaving behind the old self and all its negativism, we may rise to newness of life in you, so that we see and feel and taste and hear the wonders of our existence in the world, and live in excitement and gratitude and humility. Through Jesus Christ our Lord. Amen.

XII

The Pastor's Ten Commandments

     I. *Thou shalt love the Lord thy God with all thy heart and mind and soul, and thou shalt love thy parishioner as thyself.* This is the first rule of a good pastorate. Love is the very basis of all we do. It is both the theology and the methodology of every parish activity. It means that before anything else the pastor must be a person of prayer and devotion, feasting on the presence of God until his or her soul is completely purified of sin and hate and resentment, and can look out upon the world with inner happiness and acceptance. Everything we do ought to spring out of love—preaching, scolding, visiting, counseling, planning, greeting, hosting committee meetings, everything. When everything comes from love, evil doesn't have much of a chance in the parish.

    I remember a pastor in one of my seminary classes. We had been doing a fantasy experiment with I Corinthians 13, Paul's famous "love" chapter. I had led the class members in their imaginations to the doorstep of Paul's cottage as he was working on the chapter, and had left them there with instructions to talk with Paul about anything that was on their minds. Afterward, when we were "debriefing," this pastor said that he had had a hard time getting into the fantasy, because his mind was on an encounter he was facing at home with an unpleasant woman in his church. But, making the attempt, he had asked Paul, "Paul, what am I going to do with that woman?" "Love her," was Paul's reply, he said. "Just love her." A week later, we asked the pastor how his meeting with the woman had gone. "You know," he said, "I thought all the way home about what Paul had said, and I prayed that God would help me love her. When we came together it was different. I don't know why, but we sort of hit it off. She was a lot nicer than I thought she was. I think I did love her."

This is the way with love. It solves all problems.

II. *Thou shalt keep the worship and preaching of thy church strong and inspiring.* There is nothing our people need more than this. They need other things too, but this is central. There is in any parish a reciprocity between worship and work. That is, the better the worship, the stronger the work, and vice versa. It is an early temptation of ministers, soon after they leave seminary, to let their preparation for worship and preaching slide. They get to know their parishioners and experience a little indulgence from them; then they say, "Oh, I can get by without working so hard on my sermon and prayers this week." And, pretty soon, they are spending all their time out in the fields with the hands and none in the kitchen preparing their nourishment. It is a tragic mistake. People need to experience the Holy in worship; they need to hear the Word addressing them in terms that are incarnate for their lives. Otherwise faith soon loses its vitality and brilliance. Everything in the church becomes a cliché. That young preacher in one of David H. C. Read's books who dreamed of the perfect parish as consisting of a study where he worked all week and a tunnel leading into the pulpit, where he disgorged himself of the week's produce, was obviously wrongheaded about ministry; but so is the older preacher who thinks the perfect parish is a marketplace with no study and no pulpit. Each vision needs the other for harmony and balance. I have always thought of the strong worship service with the well-prepared sermon as the center pole holding the tent erect so that the rest of the acts can go on under the canvas without interruption. The other acts do not go on merely because the center pole is there; but they would be thrown into considerable darkness and confusion if it weren't!

III. *Thou shalt work always at the peripheries of thy congregation.* This insight, which I have cherished for years, was well articulated by Phillips Brooks, who said that the pastor can have no better instinct than that of the sheep dog, which knows to ply the edges of the flock, turning wayward sheep in toward the center. Those at the center will get along well and safely. It is the ones on the periphery we must watch out for. The pastor's temptation, of course, is to spend most of his or her time with the attractive and amiable people at the core of the church's organization and life. It is not only that these persons are the most natural and accessible objects of our attention, but, as prudence reminds us, they are the most likely judges and rewarders of our performance. But how stale and limited the church would be if it never encountered in a meaningful way the tastes and ideas of the persons on its circumference, and if these persons were never brought within the zones of power and influence in the congregation. The true richness of life lies in diversity and discovery. Christ calls to us from the boundaries of the church as much as from the center, and we are not fulfilling our mission as pastors when we devote the major portion of our energies to those who live comfortably at the center and seldom engage those at the border.

It is good pastoral practice, at least once a week, to make a special effort to get to know someone who has been only tangentially related to the congregation, or who appears to dip in and out of it like a swallow getting a drink. A little interest will often bring such persons deeper into the fellowship and enrich the life of the entire Body of Christ.

IV. *Thou shalt forever attempt to get others to do thy work.* This is not counsel to be a lazy minister. On the contrary, it often takes more energy to maneuver others into ministry than to do it yourself. But it is of vital importance, if church members are to grow in understanding and deepen their allegiance to Christ, that they learn to participate in the work of the ministry. I was once a perfectionist who believed that I ought to do myself all those things that I could do better or more efficiently than others. Now I see that what we are trying to perfect is not the discreet, individual tasks we are working at but the community of faith, and that it is best perfected by letting everyone have a part in it. The pastor needs to be like a schoolteacher who gives the children things to do and then resists the urge to do them in his or her own way. It is the children's growth that matters, not the excellence of what they produce. Perhaps the pastor can make a better speech on stewardship than one of the deacons or write a better editorial than the editor of the newsletter. That is beside the point. The deacon and the editor need to do what they can do. We should never take a straight line to a goal if a circuitous line will involve more people.

V. *Thou shalt hold on to what works and let go of what doesn't.* This is pure pragmatism, of course, and there are times when it doesn't apply, especially when principle is involved. But generally it is good advice. Pastors spend far too much time and energy trying to prop up programs that won't stand by themselves and make things work that were improperly designed in the first place. No good sales representative continues to push products that are impossible to move, and no fisherman spends inordinate amounts of time trying to untangle snagged lines. The smart pastor soon learns to say of a project that wouldn't fly, "Well, chalk that one up to experience and let's pour our energies into something else."

One of my most dismal failures at my present church was the formation of a PR council. We had several members connected with newspapers, magazines, public relations offices, the printing business, and other lines of communication. I had the bright idea of assembling them, dividing them into subgroups in charge of intramural publicity, extramural publicity, church publications, church stationery and bulletins, and our weekly radio broadcast. It was a brilliant plan. All the people were clever, and several were good professionals. What I didn't reckon on was that they were all very committed to their own work and weren't particularly interested in grabbing a line and running with it. We had three organizational meetings with diminishing success. By the time we had the last one, it was obvious that the council was not going to fly. It was a disaster. I finally buried it as a dead idea and went on to spend my energy among the living. Perhaps it will come back again in its own time. That is another thing.

Picasso said he never feared to paint out a color in a painting; if it belonged, it would come back. The same is true of ideas and organizations in the church. No matter how often we drop them, the good ones will come back.

VI. *Thou shalt turn every meeting, however casual or unintended, into a pastoral occasion.* I meet Mrs. Jones in the parking lot as she is coming to the church on an errand and I am going out on an errand. We exchange pleasantries, in the course of which she mentions that she has had a bladder infection and was afraid before going to the doctor that it was something worse. Last year her sister died of cancer. If I am sensitive to her feelings, and not in too big a hurry to be a pastor, I will wonder if she is not identifying with her sister's illness and having problems with death anxieties. Skillfully, but with an air of casualness, I probe her mind with a few questions and see that my suspicion is correct; she *is* worried about dying. I take a few moments to talk with her about the way we acquire anxieties after losing loved ones and then to relate some of the comforting aspects of our faith. I make a mental note to go by to see her in the near future and perhaps to take her a book that will have special meaning in her situation. I have made a pastoral contact that was almost as good as a pastoral call, and it all took less than five minutes.

If I am alert, I will make dozens of these contacts every day—in the grocery store, at the club, on the street, in the corridors of the hospital, wherever I go. And if I am of a generous nature, I won't confine them to my own church members, I'll be a pastor-at-large.

VII. *Thou shalt cherish the gifts of others and imagine ways to use them.* I don't know about you, but I have a brokering spirit. That is, I like to see people doing things they enjoy doing and do well, and I am always trying to picture new situations where they can do them. It's like running an employment service out of your hat. You keep trying to match people and jobs, and sometimes you have to invent the jobs in order to put them together. It's a wonderful penchant to have, especially in the church, for it results in all these combinations that make people happy and provide surprising advantages—real bonuses!—for everybody. I'm not as good at it as one pastor I know. He has this phenomenal ability to meet somebody for the first time, size up the person, and say, "Hey, I bet you would make a wonderful mime for our annual program for the deaf. Have you ever done any clowning?" And even though the person has never done it before, she agrees to try and turns in a sensational performance that leads to a new avocation. A large part of our job is helping people to fulfill themselves in Christ, and this means giving them things to do that will bring out their talents and permit them to relate to others in as many ways as possible. We can do it if we really care about them and the talents they have to offer to the world.

VIII. *Thou shalt publicize, publicize, publicize.* I don't mean the church and what it can do for the community, or the minister and what he or she is doing for the church. I mean the people in the church and what they are doing for one another. What they are doing is good news, and it helps offset the bad news in the world at large. No one is in a better position than the minister to know all the kind and generous acts done by people in the parish. It is therefore incumbent on the minister to be a publicist for these things.

I once met a wise little lady in North Carolina who asked the question, "Why is it that preachers don't have as much sense as a honeybee?" Honeybees, she said, flit from flower to flower, carrying sweetness from one to the other, and yet many preachers get in the pulpit and do nothing but rehearse the bad news about all that's wrong with the world around them. Enthusiasm begets enthusiasm, and if we will only take more time to puff the good things that happen, our parishes will be more positive places. I often notice, as I visit my parishioners, that nothing brightens our time together as much as some bit of news about a good deed that one person has done for another. It has an infectious quality and tends to beget other good deeds. Similarly, I always try to mention in my pastor's paragraphs and from the pulpit the wonderful little things people do for the church. The more I talk about these things, the more people do them. "Oh, isn't that nice!" they say; and then they too are in the mood to do something nice.

IX. *Thou shalt always be positive and upbuilding in thy speech and attitudes.* For years I have been nourished by Sarah Orne Jewett's little short story, "Miss Tempy's Watchers." Miss Tempy, a maiden lady who lived in a small village in Maine, has died, and the "watchers" are two women who sit in her parlor through the night, recalling bits and pieces of her life. In the course of their conversation they praise the wonderful quince jelly Miss Tempy made and distributed among friends every year. One woman expresses amazement that her lone old quince tree continued to bear fruit year after year. "She just *expected* that thorny old thing into blooming," remarks the other. There is a world of good advice for pastors in that statement. It is in our power to coax a lot of thorny old things into blooming. We simply have to have the right attitudes. People get tired of their own negativism. We can help them cultivate a spirit of affirmation and joy. It will not be hard, if we live by the first commandment, to love God with all our hearts and minds and souls. Love will imbue us with a sense of grace and mystery, and these will characterize everything we say and do.

There was an old minister in Nova Scotia who was preparing to retire. The people in one of his earlier pastorates wrote him and asked: "Would you come and settle among us? We feel that we'd be a better community and better neighbors for having a man like you living among us." This is the power of a positive faith. It makes an enormous difference in people's lives. They soon catch the enthusiasm of a higher way of life and want to follow it themselves. From the pulpit, in the counseling session, while walking along the street, we can help create a new climate for love and generosity among our people, and Christ will reign among us in glorious wonder!

X. *Thou shalt remember to say thanks for the gift of a pastorate.* When all is said and done, what richer place could there be for us to live our lives? Imagine having a family of hundreds of people, all caring about you and the way you feel, inviting you into the inner sanctums of their lives, sharing their sorrows and joys with you, listening to your speeches, holding you up to God each day in prayer, and trying in their various ways to help you do your job. There is no other calling in the world quite like it. Where else could we feel as satisfied about the worth of what we are doing? Oh, it is natural to have our times of discouragement and despondency. If we didn't, we would think it was time to hold the devil's funeral. But on the whole it is hard to picture a profession in which the rewards are so rich and heartfelt. Perhaps this is why, all over the country, the median age of seminary students is constantly going up. More and more persons in other professions have found those professions empty of inner satisfaction and are leaving them to enter

The Tender Shepherd

the ministry. A friend of mine who is a stockbroker recently called to say he is forsaking his business for the ministry. "I have made a lot of money," he said, "but I have found that money is not what I want out of life." I wager he will find what he wants in the pastorate. I have. When someone asked me the other day, "Do you miss academia?" I replied, "No, not for a minute. This is the richest life I could ever imagine!"

cover photograph—Sid Dorris
cover and book design—Steve Laughbaum
assistance from—Karen Trogdon